EXUBERANCE

EXUBERANCE

A Philosophy of Happiness

Paul Kurtz

P Prometheus Books
Buffalo and New York City

158.1
K96e

Published 1977 by Prometheus Books
1203 Kensington Avenue, Buffalo, New York 14215

Library of Congress Catalog Card Number: 77-73847
ISBN 0-87975-091-X

Impact Series

Printed in the United States of America

185489

For:
Martin and Sarah
Who gave me life

Contents

Preface / Bursting at the Seams

There must be something wrong with me. I am happy, exuberant. This has been true for as long as I can remember. Am I sick? Those around me seem to moan and complain, while I usually wake up singing and am joyful throughout the day. Life is so wonderful. I feel literally as if I am bursting at the seams.

Why am I happy? What does it mean to be satisfied—deeply—with life?

I ask this not only because I wish to plumb the depths of my own being but because I want others to learn what I have learned, intuitively and analytically, about the fullness of life and the opportunities for happiness.

I do not deny that despair, unreason, anxiety, meaninglessness lurk somewhere in the background. Yet, these passions and problems have never bothered me as they have others. I have never, or rarely ever, been overwhelmed by despondency or *angst*. I have never lost my verve for life or the strong motivation to persevere.

I am told that menopause or prostate trouble await

everyone, and perhaps someday I will encounter periods of depression. Perhaps I will undergo some great tragedy yet to unfold. Perhaps my accounting is still to take place, and I owe the universe some suffering. I have had my share of troubles. Yet they never were able to bow my back or buckle me under. I even found such traumatic experiences not without significance. Misery and pathos add intense, if dissonant, qualities to life experience. Others often emphasize the negative side of life. I accentuate the positive aspects. I am oblivious to the pall of gloom.

Instead I invariably feel exhilarated and find that there are not enough hours in a day to do all the things that I want to do. I am confronted by so many good things, interesting experiences, exciting possibilities. I want to do them all. I approach each with excitement. I admire Beethoven, whose paeans of *freude* provide my theme song: joy, joy, joy!; Picasso, whose intensity exudes hope, confidence, and vitality in his works of art; Michelangelo, who tempts nature with his daring and eloquent feats of artistic grandeur; Gulbenkian, the fabulous oil mogul, who when asked what he liked best replied, "everything!"; and Bertrand Russell, who lived fully as both a rational and a passionate being.

There are alternative ideals that have been drawn in human history, all promising the "good life." Is the humanistic model that I am presenting applicable to everyone? Or is it possible only for a small majority, a creative elite, Abraham Maslow's few self-actualizers—healthy, joyful achievers? In my view, although the full life is at root the heroic one, it expresses the essence of life itself; and this element is essential to the growth of human civilization. Without creative audacity, the drama of human history could not have developed as it did.

There are, as I have said, other ethical models that

compete for our attention. There is the ideal life of the so-called religious saint: ethically motivated, self-sacrificing and ascetic, full of faith and virtue, dominated by over-belief and repression. Or there is the life of the contemplative meditator: withdrawn from the world of affairs into an inner world of expanded consciousness, whether rational or transcendental in emphasis. At the other extreme the life of the pleasure seeker beckons: suckling rosebuds and breasts, seeking sensual pleasures and hedonic tones. Against that stands the life of the stoic: wishing to suppress pain and sorrow and cultivating an attitude of indifference. Always with us is the conventional establishmentarian—whether bourgeois, bureaucrat, housewife, or soldier—satisfying the traditional mores, fulfilling his tasks, doing one's duty in terms of his or her social station. And in opposition is the revolutionary: overwhelmed with the need for sacrifice and dedicated to the cause of utopian justice.

Some might say that the model of the good life that I have discovered is not to everyone's liking. Some may find it too difficult for them or too full of bravado. Perhaps one's proclivities in this direction are a function of his personality, and to some extent are even genetic. Thus, not everyone will find the activistic life suited to him or her. Yet, I believe that it is possible for many or most human beings to find some merit in the active life. For its chief excellences are courage, the willingness to dare, self-power, resourcefulness, creativity, and intelligence; and these qualities, though they play a role in daily life, are essential for any grand human achievement. Indeed, in each of the alternative models such qualities must be present to some extent if we are to live and function. It is simply a question of emphasis. If we are to proclaim a way of life, create something different, bring into being a new idea or invention, or forge a frontier, then we need to dream, take a chance, seize an opportunity. These are the qualities that are uniquely and superbly human, the risk-taking that makes possible the great human thrust.

It is not the "human predicament" about which we should worry. Those who emphasize "the human condition" are often dominated by forlornness, fear and trembling (the "Augustinian-Kierkegaardian syndrome"), and the mistaken belief that salvation comes from the passive mood—from dependence on and acquiescence to the divine. Rather, we need to underscore the activist frame, which alone makes possible those social conditions from which a transcendental lotus-eater can withdraw. By *activist frame* I refer to the dominant virtues of modern man: the willingness to take destiny in one's own hands, to tempt fate and to turn it about to suit himself. It is not the quiet release from decision, action, passion, or torment that is the goal of my life, but striving, seeking, meeting challenges, and overcoming obstacles. It is this that gives my life its special zest and vitality. It is this that makes me say that I am bursting at the seams.

Some will demur, saying that I am merely glorifying the values that dominate American society; that is, the achievement motive, success, pragmatic doing. And these values, we are told, may now be in eclipse, ephemeral expressions of a phase of human history that will pass— much the same as Aristotle's *Ethics* expressed the virtues of Hellenistic culture, Marcus Aurelius the values of Rome's, Aquinas the mood of medieval religiosity, or Bentham the utilitarian calculus of nineteenth-century Britain. Granted that our values reflect our cultural bias, so that we cannot disentangle from them entirely. Yet the heroic virtues that attempt to bend nature to our will, to express the stout spine, strong heart, or firm jaw transcend our culture and typify resilient characteristics of the human enterprise. These Promethean virtues expressed strong impulses in the pagan hearts of the Greeks and Romans; they reappeared during the Renaissance and modern times (in opposition to the Christian virtues of submissiveness and piety); and they were proclaimed anew by Nietszche at the beginning of our century. They are, in the final analysis, the qualities that make possible human achievement in every field of endeavor: art, science, industry, commerce, politics, civilization itself. They are central to the humanist frame.

It is audacity that distinguishes the human response from that of other forms of life on this planet. Man is intrepid, insolent, and impudent. He seeks to break loose from the constraints imposed by nature. He is high-spirited, restless, adventuresome, inquiring, inventive. Man is condemned to invent his own future; he is responsible for what he will become; he is forever full of hopes and aspirations, plans and projects. He is always involved in a process of discovery and creativity, seeking new paths for joyous existence. Man simply cannot acquiesce to the universe, nor is he content merely to fulfill his nature; he constantly strives to exceed himself and nature by bringing forth from his imagination creative modes of thought, new artifacts and inventions that did not previously exist in nature (tools, instruments, symbols, works of art, objects, machines, institutions, and organizations of all sorts). He does not merely discover what nature is but adds new forms and combinations to it. It is in the agony and joy of work that he truly achieves his grandeur and forges his destiny.

The meaning of life is not, in my view, to be found by withdrawing from its challenges, contemplating the universe in mystical transcendence, fulfilling our duties by moral sacrifice, or even achieving self-actualization; rather, it is created by us as we reach out, voyage, and adventure. In this process lies the drama, excitement, and exaltation of living the full life. Life has no meaning per se; it only presents opportunities for us to seize and act upon.

Part I / Activity

One / Power

I

If we are to achieve joyful exuberance, the first point to recognize is that human beings *can* have some power and control of their own destinies. We can live a full life, but only if we are able to expand our sense of power, not necessarily over other humans, but of ourselves. But, we may ask what is the full extent of human power? Dare one exaggerate his capabilities without risking psychological defeat? It is well and good to emphasize the potentialities for creative autonomy, but should we not recognize that there are boundaries restricting what we can do? Is it not foolhardy to adopt the audacious stance, to proclaim the power of choice, to tempt nature or stand against the universe, seeking to bend it to our will, when all of our plans will be defeated in the end—by death, if by nothing else?

Life teaches the bitter lesson that the fondest of human dreams are often shattered. We learn the sorrows of unexpected tragedies, accidents, disease, pain, failure, defeat, conflict, and that the obdurate realities of nature often frustrate our deepest desires and play havoc with our best-laid plans. Certainly we can dream, but we can never match our dreams with realities. Nature constantly resists human efforts and often subdues them.

The religious consciousness is aware of the failures and defeats of life, particularly of the facts of human transience and death—and we are faced with the problem of evil: this is a vale of tears. How live in the face of adversity? How forbear when the cruel twists of fate can destroy us: a premature death, an unforeseen natural disaster, a plane crash, a sudden heart attack? A slight miscalculation can wreck the noblest of human plans.

How bear the slings of outrageous fortune? How does a lonely individual face the taunts and torments of existential reality? How can one live in the face of the overwhelming sense that there are vast powers in society and the universe at large is beyond his control?

The Stoics offered consolation by cultivating an inward attitude of apathy or indifference. They were impressed by the "inevitable necessity of all things" and by our own insignificance in the face of it.

Epictetus, a former Roman slave, begins the *Enchiridion* by saying:

> "There are things which are within our power, and there are things which are beyond our power. Within our power are opinion, aim, desire, aversion, and, in one word, whatever affairs are our own. Beyond our power are body, property, reputation, office, and, in a word, whatever are not properly our own affair. Now the things within our power are by nature free, unrestrained, unhindered; but those beyond our power are weak, dependent, restricted, alien. . . . Aiming, therefore, at such great things, remember that you must not allow yourself any inclination, however slight, toward the attainment of the others; but that you must entirely quit

some of them, and for the present postpone the rest. . . .
And if it concerns anything beyond our power, be prepared
to say that it is nothing to you. Remove (the habit of) aversion, then, from all things that are not within our power,
and apply it to things undesirable which are within our
power."[1]

Living in a vast empire, seemingly beyond anyone's
control, the Roman Stoic, whether emperor or slave, felt
that he had to perform such duties as were expected of him.
He could not retreat from the world, as did the Epicurean.
He could withdraw instead into himself by the suppression
of unnecessary feelings of involvement. He could lessen
anxiety and worry about the unexpected tragedies. There is
an important element of reflective awareness here, and it
suggests a kind of nobility of spirit. Yes, we say, we need the
courage to bear adversity, to go through life without being
crushed by its misfortunes. All wise persons learn that there
are some things over which they have some control, and that
there are some things far beyond human control, but that
we can contain our inward thoughts about them. It is
important that one recognize that tragic events occur: the
death of a child, the defeat of one's country, the failure of a
crop.

Yet there can also be an overemphasis on passive acceptance. The Stoic solution was to "follow the way of
nature" in order to achieve virtue. But modern man has
learned that nature is not fixed and society not closed to
human purpose and that we are able to modify the natural
world and reform social institutions.

We have discovered that there often are powers that we
have though we may be unaware of them, that situations

1. *Enchiridion*, translated by Thomas W. Higginson (Liberal Arts Press,
Bobbs Merrill, N.Y., 1948), pp. 17-18.

have latent possibilities, that there are untapped potentialities that can be actualized, that one can bring into being
new instruments to achieve one's desires, and that one can
vastly extend one's range of interests and activities.

II

The development of modern science and technology
marks a radical break with the past, for it makes possible
an enormous enlargement of human powers.

For the philosophers and scientists of Greece and
Rome and the philosophers and theologians of the Middle
Ages, the goal was to try to make the universe intelligible to
thought. Even a figure such as Spinoza, serving as a bridge
between the Middle Ages and modern science, was impressed by the order of nature. The highest human good
and the source of blessedness and salvation was for him the
intellectual love of God or nature, an appreciation of its
logical structure. Joy was in knowing that the vast panorama
of events fits a marvelous causal order and that man is part
of the scheme of things.

For Bacon, however, knowledge is power. It is not
enough to understand the universe; we must apply our
knowledge for human use. If the Greeks developed a
theoretical approach to nature, we have developed an
experimental one. Thus modern technology is an effort to
apply the principles of the sciences to practical uses; and
modern man has learned that knowledge is an instrument
and force and that he can do things with it. It is Western
man who has had strong confidence in his own powers—
much more so than those in the underdeveloped societies,
who too often believe that you cannot change anything.

It is not enough to behold in mystic vision or rational
insight the wondrous order of nature, but to use this knowl-

edge to satisfy our interests and goals and to create new ones. With scientific knowledge many of the mysterious tragedies that befall human beings—disease, accidents, premature death, famine—can now be averted. We can understand their causes, and we have a method of correction and cure. Thus our sense of power is for us far greater than that in earlier centuries. Knowledge is not a sign of the inevitable necessity of all things but a clue to the pregnant potentialities that we can unlock and the vast new powers that we can develop. As man enters the Space Age, the possibilities of adventure for the soaring human spirit are virtually unlimited.

Many people feel that modern technology has now gone too far, that we have opened a Pandora's box that can destroy us, that technology is irretrievably polluting the environment, and that it is a new demon that we must guard against.

I note these familiar facts because it is our sense of power, freedom, and autonomy that is at issue. A person cannot be audaciously happy unless he has a sense that he can guide and control his life and that of his society. Courage and persistent effort are possible only in this perspective.

If one believes that the world is predetermined and that his destiny and fate are beyond his control, then his response is to seek some measure of peace from the forces that would dominate him. He can know God and submit to his power in love and adoration, accept the "inevitable necessity of all things," or seek release in mystic contemplation; but his own efforts and concerns are of little avail. Fatalistically he says, "Whatever will be will be," and he is unwilling and unable to resist the tide of events. Thus there is in an extreme form a deep-seated religious sense of our powerlessness, helplessness, impotence: one can only prostrate oneself before nature or God or the universe.

Yet the full life is tied up with a sense in which one is aware of his own power as a person; that is, the belief that one *can* control or influence one's life to some extent, that one *can* modify or redirect the forces about one, that there is some energy at one's disposal to do so, and that one can take pride in achieving what one sets out to do. Call it naive optimism, if you will, but it is the central humanistic virtue.

III

Any theory, whether based on religion or science, that denies voluntary human choices or action flies in the face of human experience. We have power over our conduct to the extent to which our behavior is motivated; that is, insofar as our choices are our own, and follow from our own wishes and desires, plans and interests. In classical philosophical language, our behavior is free if the moving principle is within us rather than being caused by external forces or unconscious drives. Our purposes are influenced and modified, of course, by the conditions under which we act; yet at the same time we have something to say about how we act, and at the very least, can alter the conditions under which we act.

There are two key factors in a purposive process: (a) we have an idea or wish as an end goal, and (b) we engage in activity or work to bring it about. Creative thinking continually intervenes in the initiating of new goals, in the kinds of adaptive behavior that we engage in to achieve our ends, and in the invention of new means and instruments to bring them about. In all of these senses man is not a passive recipient but a dynamic agent. He has something to say about his future, for he can think up new projects and plans, create organizations and techniques that did not exist before, and rearrange and reorder the materials of nature in novel ways. His ability to do this depends only upon whether or not he has a rich and fertile imagination.

We can see creativity at work in the public and private lives of individuals as they introduce goals and plans and go about resolving them. Thinking is both imaginative-creative and coping-adjustive. Teleonomic choice is the fundamental process in human life; that is, what will happen in the future is a result of the purposes that we initiate and try to bring about: going to the supermarket to purchase groceries, enrolling in law school, building a condominium, developing a career, writing an article, moving to Arizona, investing in the commodity exchange, or helping to build a space colony.

Now some of the things that we resolve to do, we can do. There are few obstacles; the means are readily available; the end is clearly in view. Our daily decisions fit into this means-end continuum. I decide to wallpaper the bedroom, and so I select the paper, get the brushes and paste, and go merrily about my business, completing the job in one afternoon. Similar factors apply for choices of longer duration. I plant a vegetable garden in the spring, care for it throughout the summer, and harvest it in the fall. Or I begin a book, spending many months or years researching and writing it. Now in some of the projects that I wish to bring to fruition, I may encounter great difficulties. The glue is too thin and the paper peels. There is a hail storm and my vegetables are ruined. I am unable to complete my book, due to distractions.

Often I may experience great obstacles: the means I use may be inadequate, consequences that were unforeseen may ensue, contingent events may intrude. Indeed, that is often the plight of the human condition. The path may not be easy and smooth, but rutted and full of dangers. Some people seem to have an excess of "bad luck"; a whole set of circumstances may trip them up; they may make blunders. Thus the dreams they cherish may not come true, though those of their neighbors do. Their plans may be thwarted by natural forces—the resistance of brute facts—or by human and social forces beyond their control. Woodrow Wilson was unable to complete his term as president because of ill health, or to see his belief in a League of Nations bear fruit in the United States. Franklin Roosevelt was felled by a fatal stroke on the eve of victory in war. Lyndon Johnson was unable to bring a close to the Vietnam war; every policy he initiated seemed to spell disaster. Robert Kennedy was struck down by an assassin's bullet, cutting short his drive for presidential power. Richard Nixon and Spiro Agnew, at the height of their power, after an unprecedented electoral victory, were brought down by forces that they were unable to master or comprehend.

The frustration of our plans constantly tests us. Not all of the things that we want can come true. Our fantasies exceed our capacities, our best-laid plans sometimes are destroyed by fortune and the tide of events. We may encounter unrequited love, electoral defeat, financial ruin, public ridicule and shame, illness, or we may perform badly. These are the realities of the human condition, and everyone—the great and the small—suffers them to some degree. The whole point to life is this: Can I overcome the adversity, or will I be crushed by it? Eli Black, head of the vast business conglomerate General Brands, leaped to his death in the midst of financial difficulties. Anthony Eden resigned from office after the Suez fiasco. General Robert E. Lee surrendered, recognizing that the Southern cause was hopeless. Golda Meir gave up the reigns of power in Israel.

In one sense what will happen depends on the strength

of our will and our willingness to persevere. The hero of Ernest Hemingway's *The Old Man and the Sea* is determined to snare his fish and hold on to him at all costs, in spite of tremendous difficulties, and in the end he succeeds. Napoleon, after being exiled to Elba, returned to lead a mighty army to Paris for one last attempt at conquest, and all the monarchs of Europe shuddered at his daring. Lindbergh flew across the Atlantic alone on an uncharted path. Beethoven continued composing though he was crushed by an onrushing deafness. Helen Keller learned to communicate and to develop as a person in spite of being deaf, dumb, and blind.

The world mourns a departed leader and applauds the hero as a public figure. But we all know that our private lives are filled with the same vivid qualities and that the human adventure includes adversity, defeat, and frustration, as well as success and victory.

It is the drive of the individual, the unflinching persistence of the will, and the enduring strength of character that is the dynamic factor in achievement. We don't always succeed; we need to adjust our dreams, learn from our mistakes, adapt to circumstances. Human intelligence and courage need to be artistically blended by creative endurance.

The achievement motive can motivate strongly. But in addition to ability, sagacity, skill and training, success requires some resolve and patience, tenacity and persistence, and the absence of excessive remorse. In a sense, then, whether we achieve our ends is a function of whether we have tapped our power. Why some persons have confidence in their powers while others do not is a difficult question. But the actual pursuit of the exuberant life depends upon the quality of boldness, and it involves the conviction that if you try something you can do it. One phrase that has remained with me since elementary school is my teacher's early advice to me: "Never say you *can't*. Get rid of that word from your vocabulary." Others have agreed. "They can because they think they can," observes Virgil. "No one knows what he can do till he tries," agrees Publius.

Why do some men lack the ability to try, while others are willing to take chances and risks? Some individuals have learned life's lesson, "nothing ventured, nothing gained." Yet others will never venture and will instead prefer safety and security. Some are overcome by indecision. Unable and unwilling to decide, they let events slip through their fingers, impotent to act or to conquer them. In the process they become mere spectators, rather than actors, debilitated by uncertainty and indecisiveness, overwhelmed by caution and trembling.

Fear is the source of human weakness, and insofar as one is afraid to act, to undertake something new, one is unable to become an autonomous person. "He who hesitates is lost." Yet many not only hesitate, they never act. Human beings are divided into two classes: those who are willing to act and those who are not, the courageous and the fearful, the achievers and the might-have-beens.

Often related to this attitude of fear is one of self-hatred, which only exacerbates a person's feelings of impotence. Some degree of self-respect and self-love is essential for any human accomplishment. But if we inwardly believe that we will fail in what we do, or if we are afraid to act, the result is often demeaning to oneself. And as life goes on and we get older, our sense of self-worth may be further weakened. Lacking confidence in what we can achieve, we lack confidence in our own worth as a person; we are inwardly self-critical and self-destructive; we turn upon ourselves, and the process of self-immolation feeds upon itself.

The opposite of fear and impotence is a feeling of personal worth and power; only these feelings permit us to continue to develop our sense of power. One can overcome excessive stoic resignation about the universe or one's personal limitations only if one has a sense of one's own proper freedom. One can extend the limits of one's own action and of the things within one's power. To be human is to be free; freedom is the chief source of human fulfillment. But what does it mean to be free? It does not mean that my actions are uncaused or unconditioned by events around me. It does not mean that I can act counter to the deterministic forces in nature. It means only that I am to some extent self-determined and that what happens to me, to those about me, and to my society also depends upon my efforts and actions, on what I add to the situation, and on what I decide to do. I am thus responsible in part for my destiny. Impotence signifies that I am unable to do anything, that I cannot succeed, that my efforts will fail. Potency points to the belief that I do have the capacity and opportunity to act in the world. Powerlessness is corroding and destructive of human personality; potency, a dynamic source of vigor and motivation. To say that I am free means that I have my own ideals of what the future should be like and that I can take steps to realize them in the world of action. *My* ideas have consequences. *I* can change things, alter them for the better. I *can* achieve the good life for myself.

IV

Obviously there are limits to what one can do. Those who refuse to recognize limits are foolish; they may be inordinately power-hungry or completely impractical. Overweening ambition or egoistic omnipotence is as much out of touch with the world as self-defeating impotence, for nature dictates that if we are to succeed in our goals that we have a realistic appraisal of what is objectively possible. We learn from bitter experience that impulsive behavior, imprudent policies, or taking unnecessary chances may have disastrous consequences. If one's dreams are not based upon a cognitive analysis of the real world, they are likely to be shattered. Practical wisdom can help us to ferret out nonsensical proposals from hard-nosed ones. Merely to want something and to resolve to get it is never enough. We need intelligence to appraise the circumstances in the situation in which we act, both as to the possibilities *and* the limits. Of course, we may be lucky; but to gamble constantly in life is to risk the probability of being crushed by the wheels of fortune. One's risks must be hedged. A risk should be taken only if there is a presumption of success. To dash in without planning and without properly examining the terrain is not a sign of bravery but of ignorance. As Aristotle pointed out, courage must be harmonized with intelligence; without it, it is simply rashness or foolishness. One can be the master of his fate—yes. But one should not be so childish as to come unprepared. Courage without calculation is stupidity. Thus our plans and projects often are impossible or unlikely to succeed, and it is wiser not to act—we learn that from experience. Freedom does not mean that I can do whatever I want, only that what I choose to do or not to do is a function of a deliberative process. And deliberation is a major ingredient in making actions succeed. Choices that are a product of a process of reflective inquiry are most likely more effective than those that are not. They are choices based upon a consideration of the facts of the case, of the possibilities and limitations, the means at one's disposal, the alternatives that are available and can be created by me, and an appraisal of the likely consequences of various courses of action.

I may choose not to act, to forbear, to hold back, to adopt a cautious stance. But such a reflective choice also expresses my power as an autonomous agent. The converse of inaction, so typical of the powerless, is hyperaction. This can become an illness: to try to run in many directions at the same time, to refuse to stop to catch one's breath, to be continually high on projects without end, not to be able to sit still a minute, to begin new tasks without finishing previous ones. If there is a vice that most threatens the hyperactive personality, it is the attempt to do too many things at the same time. Some men are able to succeed: they become the Leonardos of action; others become merely squanderers undertaking too many projects, but doing none of them well. They never seem able to enjoy life. Always on the run, they are unable to savor the delicacies and subtleties of experience. They are vulgar pragmatists, judging life only by its consequences in action, but forgetting that many of the good things of life should be intrinsically enjoyed for their own sake, and that utilitarian values can often smother sensual delight, the joys of repose and rest, meditation and tranquillity.

The end of life is not simply action for its own sake; the full life involves an integration of action with other phases of experience and an appreciation for hedonic tones and erotic sensitivities. Thus one should not do merely for the sake of doing, but doing should be related to other qualities of immediate experience, which can interpenetrate harmoniously in a full life. Action will lose its intrinsic worth unless it is related to the unified functioning of consciousness. One of the major sources of unhappiness for the hyperactive person is the inability to enjoy life's pleasures. One should live not simply to act, but to appreciate the joys of experience. There is also some danger that the strenuous mood of affirmation and achievement, in blotting out the virtues of rest and repose, may make the action-oriented person more liable to stress. Prey to ambition, overwhelmed by conflict and competition, such a person is especially prone to anxiety conflicts. It is important, therefore, that the action-oriented person place his action in a broader framework. Of significance here is the need to cultivate some stoic virtues, for individuals who play the game of life so hard that they cannot bear to lose are often consumed by anxieties of failure. Granted that one should try hard; yet one should not be overly apprehensive of defeat, nor allow self-recrimination or self-flagellation to torment himself. It is not the active life but the worry that may accompany it that is destructive to balance and health. One should strive to succeed, but if one fails—well, the appropriate response is to make allowances and say that one will do better next time. To be able to withstand adversities, to survive psychologically in spite of failures is the best preventative of this kind of stress. To be able to achieve some self-acceptance, one must to some extent be able to see oneself in perspective, as a bystander, to laugh at one's mistakes, and also to be able to forgive them. Those who are excessively hard on themselves because of their failings not only are difficult to live with, they can't live with themselves.

The Stoics were mistaken in their view that human power is thwarted by nature—we can extend our sense of what we can do far beyond what they thought we were capable of. Yet, some Stoic consolation should still accompany our actions. Some philosophical wisdom is a necessary antidote for the vicissitudes of fortune.

V

Personal power and freedom are essential if one is to live a full and creative life. Yet the extent to which an autonomous life is possible may not depend simply upon *my* attitude and resolve, but also upon the kind of society in which I live. There are some societies and institutions that excessively smother individuality. Autonomy does not thrive where the cultural soil is alien, where there is excessive repression, a solidified class structure, strict laws, hidebound traditions, or a dominant collectivist-communal ethic. Even in closed societies there is a need to develop some talented leaders within the elite who are capable of decision and action, if they are to govern effectively, though the great mass of people may be prevented from doing so.

Thus, insofar as individual autonomy is essential for the good life, libertarian values should prevail. Social regulations though necessary, should never dampen individual choice. We surely need laws to fulfill the common good, but we need at the same time to maximize opportunities for individual achievement, allowing individuals to express their talents, interests, purposes, and careers as they see fit without excessive interference. A free man says: I cannot live in a society that unduly limits my power. I cannot breathe or create. I can thrive only where I am free to think, feel, and act in my own terms. A free society is thus a precondition for individuals being able to fully express their powers.

Regretfully, there are far too many individuals who are willing to forfeit their freedom to social demands. They lack the courage to be what they want to be because they are fearful of what others might say and are unable to withstand criticism. The superego suppresses the desire of the ego to express itself. This is due in part to the distaste that many individuals have of not being liked; this reluctance makes them easily succumb to negative criticisms. They mean well and they cannot understand why others impugn their motives.

A person needs to discover, however, that although criticisms, especially if unwarranted, may be painful at first, eventually one can learn to bear them. One should abandon the belief that one can satisfy everyone. Hopefully, we should learn to live with others harmoniously, to profit from their criticisms, where constructive, and to correct our mistakes. But we should not excessively worry about whether or not one receives universal approval, which is an impossible goal anyway. Individuals who are willing to abandon their independence also capitulate their claim to happiness. They are vanquished before the start.

Two / Ambiguity

I

Another profound source of human anxiety, hence, powerlessness, is the inability to cope with an ambiguous world. Yet a pervasive characteristic of the human universe is precisely its uncertainty. Human destiny is not fixed; it does not unfold in terms of a foreordained plan; it is open and indeterminate.

The key to life is its dramatic quality. It is charged with unexpected events, bizarre happenings; it is full of a constant stream of characters and personalities, richly diverse and idiosyncratic. One has to learn to live with dramatic suspense—not behold life as a spectator, but to participate in it lustily and mightily.

Life, however, unlike play-acting, is the *real* thing. The script has not been written beforehand; it is we who do the writing of our parts. And there are many parts that interweave and unfold. We don't know the exact ending. That is part of the excitement of living. We are forever rewriting the scenareo; and new events intrude that we did not anticipate. The full plot is always yet to unfold: it depends upon our own powers as they are spilled out into the world.

We constantly make plans for the future. We base our judgments upon past experience and future expectations. But the future we want may not come true, and we may have to readjust our sights and revise our horizons. We have to learn to face these facts. As I have said, the human universe is not predetermined, but is in part determined by us. Although there are causal conditions, patterns, and order in nature and human life in terms of which we act, there is also an element of personal choice. And there is at the same time chance and the unexpected. It is out of these three ingredients—stability and order, self-determination and choice, and chance and contingency—that the dramatic and ambiguous aspects of human life reveal themselves.

Unfortunately there are those who so emphasize the first ingredient—stability and order—that they negate the reality of the second and third. Many individuals who manifest great fear in accepting their own autonomy and power also deny that chance is real in the universe.

Broadly conceived, there is the mood that abandons human independence and power, craves security, probes existence for stability, gropes for absolute purity, searches for finality and fixity. Exuberance is closed for them. Clearly there is a psychological need in many individuals for order and certitude. Life is so full of danger that some flee into a garden of repose where there is no risk of failure nor need for effort. Three manifestations of this are the quests for God or Utopia or determinism. All three illusive quests look outside of the domain of human choice for clues to human existence, and they seek to find some secure place to anchor the evanescent character of our world.

There is, of course, ample evidence for the existence of order and stability in the universe: the seasons come and go, seedlings develop into plants, infants become adults. We discover empirically the patterns in nature and life. Science is a powerful tool for uncovering causes hidden from direct observation. We discern the causal relationships of particular events by relating them to general lawlike conditions. We could not live and act unless we presupposed some order and regularity; if all events were random and fortuitous, rational action would be impossible. But we can make predictions based upon the conjunctions of objects and events in our experience; and a body of reliable knowledge develops, enabling us to act more wisely. The growth of human knowledge expands our understanding of natural processes. The more we investigate, the wider our appreciation of the causal basis of these processes. Science does not seek an explanation of the totality of events but formulates hypotheses about specific ranges of data.

Some seek to go further and to claim that *all* events— including human events—not only manifest discernible regularities but fulfill a deeper order. Religion attributes to some Spiritual Being the ultimate source of existence. It maintains that the universe is unfolding according to a divine scheme.

The question to be raised is: What room for autonomy do we humans have in the universe, given the fact of order? Is there some freedom of choice and action? The whole of human existence points to the reality of freedom. To deny it is to substitute faith in a universal principle of determinism for the direct evidence of lived experience: the stuff of human reality is our experiences, thoughts, concepts, dreams, goals, interests, aims. Human causality is self-directed and fulfills our purposes. We function as organic mechanisms,

responding to stimuli in the external and internal environment. Yet we are also active agents; we do not simply react
passively but transact selectively and creatively to stimuli,
real and imagined.

The world we live in is rich with unique events, accidents, and novelties. It is full of surprises. Events may have
many meanings for us; what is or will happen may be unpredictable, vague, or obscure. There is often considerable
room for doubt. Change is the pervasive fact of life, and we
may be dismayed by the irregularities, by the breakdown of
old patterns in nature and society.

One can never avoid problems and difficulties in life
nor remain at dead center. Life requires ongoing effort and
exertion, in making a living, meeting new friends, falling in
love, raising children, seeing our projects through, coming
to terms with old age and death. There are uncertainties
and ambiguities in making decisions. One can never count
finally on anything. There are those who seek to escape
from this world of indeterminacy because it is for them a
source of anxiety and sorrow. Some are so bewildered by the
dramatic aspects of life, the insecurities of daily existence,
the instabilities of society, that they seek to deny the ephemeral character of experience and to flee to an eternal world
of perfection. The idea of God functions in this way for
many: He, it is said, will save us from our disappoint-
ments and miseries, restore the sick and crippled, bring
the dead back to life, overcome evil and tragedy. This is a
grand illusion in human civilization; yet it is fed by a profound hunger of the human spirit for security and certainty,
order and perfection.

Some present day utopianists in many ways share the
same psychological need as theists. Society as we know it is
corrupt, imperfect, disordered, full of conflict and strife.
The utopianist postulates another world of beneficence and

felicity; his vision promises an escape from this world of effort and toil to the world of a perfect society. Salvation is to be achieved in some future blessed state of ideal social harmony.

The utopianist masks an underlying fear about the world: his desire to totally remake it reveals his inability to function in it. Surely we wish to ameliorate social injustice. We cannot remain content with the status quo but need to introduce new plans for a better future. This is not at issue; what is, is the inability of some to accept anything in the present, living instead fixated on an ideal future. It is this mood that is pathological; and like theism, it is full of idolatry. The fellow utopianists become the new heroes who share one's vision; those who oppose them, the demons. Ideological movements express the same fear of ambiguity and the same hope for salvation as traditional religions, and they end up with the same quest for absolutes.

Yet, ambiguity and indeterminism are essential ingredients of the brew of life, whether individually or socially. To seek to separate them out would be to lose the distinctive flavor of life.

II

The question that we need to ask is: How can we learn to live with ambiguity? First, by attempting to avoid illusions as far as possible—including those about oneself—although the latter may not be completely avoidable. It is the historic myths that have been perpetuated by theism or utopianism that we especially need to overcome today—belief in a Being of which none greater can be conceived, upon whom we can rely for salvation, or belief that there is a future existence far greater than that which we now know and to which we can escape.

Religions, whether theistic or ideological, that have

looked outside of human resources for aid and succor have undermined self-reliance. Undoubtedly such religions have played a psychological role in civilization offering sustenance and comfort. But at least some individuals are able to resist their lure. If one is convinced that belief in God or Utopia is a millstone rather than a crutch, then to rid oneself of that belief is to be relieved of a burden.

One is free if he has no God-fixation to confound him, no sense of guilt about a supposed Divine Law to constrain his efforts, no false hopes of Utopia. He has an advantage over others: if he can break the chains of deception, he can have a more realistic appraisal of his own powers. He must be able to accept the universe for what it is, or can become, dependent upon what he does. Ambiguity is a fact of life that he must learn to live with, indeed, exult in.

The search for order, stability, or perfection is destined to fail in the end. For although there are some regularities in nature, creative choice is also an essential component in our life-world. History is not the operation of blind laws working themselves out in mechanical or dialectical fashion. What has or will happen depends in part upon us. We can make effective decisions. Things can turn out like we want them to; we can develop a body of prudential norms based upon practical experience. Yet we are fallible and we can make mistakes. To live and work effectively requires some intelligence and patience, qualities that we may not have in sufficient abundance. Moreover, there are other agents on the stage of social action, and it is the interaction of these many centers of choice that increases the role of the fortuitous in human affairs. Where there are many transacting agents, confusion often results. Other people may make decisions that are unpredictable or out of character, and this may distort our calculations. Thus there is always an element of incertitude in human transactions:

How will the other person react? Will he or she manifest sagacity and skill, or ignorance and cowardice? We cannot always ascertain beforehand what other persons will do. They may not know themselves. This being the case, a number of temporal categories characterize our life-world. There is some element of risk or hazard; though life manifests order and regularity, it also has an element of precariousness, indefiniteness, unclarity, inexactitude.

The concatenation of events in nature introduces other imponderables. The elements of ambiguity thus are compounded by natural forces as well, for there are always novel and contingent events that intrude to disturb our expectations: a flood, rampage, cyclone or fire, a volcanic eruption or earthquake, an accident or affliction. Not all events are predictable; nature has its own dramas. The improbable sometimes occurs.

Scientific determinists deny this. They insist that if we knew all of the causes operative in nature, we could predict all future events. But this is an article of faith. Determinism seems more appropriately to be a convenient rule of inquiry rather than a generalization of fact. Clearly, we should continue to look for explanations of why events occur; we wish to make predictions based upon our knowledge of antecedent conditions. We cannot say that an event is uncaused simply because we do not know what its causes are. With the progressive development of scientific knowledge, we gradually discover the relevant causes.

But even if scientific determinism were true (I would accept weak, but not strong, determinism), that would not mean the end of ambiguity. For we are talking about human knowledge, and our knowledge itself is never infallible; nor can we say that it has ever reached its ultimate formulation. Taking inventory of our universe—human, cultural, moral—we find both kinds of conditions: order and disorder, continuity and discontinuity, pattern and rupture, regularity and chaos, law and creativity.

As seen from our perspective, it is we who are uncertain, not nature. Nature is surely not conscious or purposive. Yet, from the standpoint of nature, indeterminacy and chance may be real facts; for there is a continuing interaction of multiple series of causality, and what will finally ensue may be different from what has occurred before. The data from evolution suggests the reality of novel emergences, as new forms of life appear and others disappear. The facts of human history also abundantly demonstrate the existence of contingencies. Whether chance and indeterminancy are real facts of nature is a metaphysical question that cannot finally be settled here. What does seem fairly evident is that science will not eradicate ambiguity entirely from our lives.

<h1 style="text-align:center">III</h1>

Thus ambiguities are indelible to the human condition, and we need to accept that fact and learn to live with and enjoy it. Indeed, contemplating a completely unambiguous world of certainty raises the question of whether we would want it if we could have it. Would it not denude life of its excitement and drama?

Ambiguity goes hand in hand with skepticism. It has at least two positive functions: first, it slakes our curiosity and interest. Doubt is essential for learning, for we begin to inquire usually as a result of being puzzled. Without puzzlement inquiry would not be initiated. If we were always certain, there would be no need for research and investigation. The absolutist does not doubt his principles, and so he is reluctant to engage in fresh inquiry. Knowledge grows out of a need to reestablish some harmony in situations in which there is doubt or confusion.

Second, ambiguity is pivotal in the arena of decision and action where we are faced with a continuing range of opportunities and possibilities. If a course of action is predetermined, if something is done for us, if we simply respond habitually, there is no need to choose. But we deliberate because we have some doubt about what to do. We may be faced by conflicting meanings. Ambiguity leads us to explore new options; it may involve experiment, ingenuity, innovation.

Human power takes on special meaning in the context of ambiguity; faced with alternatives we express a preference. We cull out and discriminate, divide and glean. We select what we find desirable, worthy, valuable. It is human initiative and drive in conduct that stabilizes the situation for us. Thus intelligence and power convert an ambiguous context into one that is unambiguous and clear; action restores continuity and order.

Now, it is apparent that some people hate to choose. They can't make up their minds. They are forever baffled and confused. Always in a quandary, they prefer to avoid having to decide; indecision, vacillation, and hesitation are their constant companions. Such people fear ambiguity; it means that they have to choose when they don't want to.

How can one develop a taste for independence in choice? The willingness to tolerate ambiguities and to find them interesting and challenging is related to our ability to resolve them. We can't remain endlessly content with an ambiguity, simmering and stewing forever in doubt. We want to resolve it by initiating creative thought and decisive action. But once we have solved one puzzle, we must be willing to entertain others that may arise and resolve them as well.

There is a constant flux between ambiguity and resolution, success and defeat. We wish to be effective in what we do, but we should not be overwhelmed by adversity. Indeed, learning to adjust to failure is essential for life. We need to learn from our mistakes, perhaps to experience remorse, but not at the price of complete inaction. One can never be vanquished entirely. Some of my projects may give way, but there are always new ones to undertake. I need to be willing to take new risks, to venture forth again. It is not only ambiguity that I must learn to cope with, but defeat; if I cannot, my life will truly be fixated in a state of despair.

In the last analysis, an indefinite world of opacity and chance is clarified and ordered by human choice: it is intelligence and power that intervene. We don't let things take their natural course; rather we seek to modify them and to turn them to our own ends, to make them serve our needs. Humans do not exist to contemplate the universe, to suffer its indignities, but to bring into being a new universe of objects and events that did not exist before we entered on the scene. Man is creator in his own right, initiating purposes and bringing them into being by his own powers of intelligence and effort. This is the highest source of a purposeful life that is overflowing with joy and zest.

Three / Creative Work

I

→ Work is the fullest expression of human power. It is the means, short range and long, by which we achieve our aspirations and desires. It can be the deepest source of satisfaction.

What should be the role of work in our lives? Should we work to live or live to work? Many persons feel that they must work in order to survive, and they find such work burdensome. According to the Old Testatment, when God expelled Adam and Eve from the Garden of Eden, their punishment was that they had to labor to gain the necessities of life. God condemned Adam and his descendents to a life of arduous toil, admonishing: "In the sweat of thy face shalt thou eat bread." From this perspective, work is drudgery. Humans have always engaged in exhausting and back-breaking labor: tilling the soil, digging for water, building shelters, hunting, making tools, chopping wood, weaving, mending from dawn to dusk. In modern urban, industrial society, work is often viewed solely as a means: we work to earn money with which we may buy things that we need or want. Workers often loathe the kind of work they do. It is stigmatized as boring and oppressive. They are forced to work merely to receive money to buy things and to do what they really want to do. The most depressing picture of oppressive work is the life of the common unskilled day laborer—the hewer of wood and drawer of water, the coal miner and steelworker, the longshoreman and sweatshop seamstress.

For Marx the chief source of human alienation is the fact that we are compelled to engage in oppressive labor. Such labor does not provide humans with the opportunity for free growth and development, or for sufficient leisure and enjoyment. He said that workers were forced to toil incessantly, day in and day out, and they still were condemned to a life of poverty and deprivation. Marx thought it unfair that human beings had to work for others, who enjoyed the fruits of their labor. He thought that the key to human liberation was to restructure the economic system and the conditions under which labor takes place. Only by doing so could we hope to become autonomous and creative.

When we are required to engage in activities that we do not wish to do, when we detest the means or are made to fulfill ends that are not our own, then work becomes mere drudgery. There are certain ends that society wishes to achieve. These involve the social production of goods and the organization of services. Where the ends to be achieved are not a person's directly, and when he works for others in order to fulfill their purposes, he may find it physically and psychologically tedious.

There is another sense of work, however, that is essential to the good life; it involves creative activity and is not considered onerous or boring. I am referring to those forms of activity that we willingly work at, through tasks that we want to do, and where we exert effort gladly to realize goals of which we approve.

The most stimulating kind of life is one in which individuals do what they want to do. A person's life may be spent in a state of idleness or leisure, where he or she does little or nothing, or it can involve excitation and activity. Voluntary activity may involve creative efforts to fulfill our purposes. When we engage in voluntary activities, our life is more satisfying.

Some of the things that we do we are in a sense compelled to, like eating, drinking, or urinating; that is, we feel constrained to act by hunger, thirst, or some other biological urge. Or we may be compelled to work to feed and clothe our family. Thus we may get a job in a factory or an office, and though we may not like the kind of work we do, we must of necessity undertake it in order to sustain ourselves.

Some of the things that we do, however, freely express our own genuine purposes, such as growing a flower garden. One may love beautiful begonias, and so purchase bulbs, plant them, cultivate the soil, and care for them daily. This may involve hard work. Yet one may enjoy it because it expresses one's own interests. A day laborer, hired to tend to someone else's flower garden, may find the work boring; if he does it for himself, he may find it more gratifying.

The distinctive spark of human greatness is creative imagination—the ability to introduce new concepts and ideals and to expend the effort to achieve them. We can dare to dream, we can institute new forms, we can initiate new projects. Where our goals are humdrum, we simply do what others have done, and our work is repetitive. But where our goals are novel and grandiose, our work can become exceptional and originative.

Herein lies the opportunity and challenge. Here work can be truly artistic, for we have a vision of the possible; our activities are all directed to achieve our ideal. The first explorer through the bush may find it full of unexpected dangers; yet he daringly forges the first trail. Those who follow him may find it less interesting.

Thus we may talk about three forms of work, in ascending order of interest and excitement:

1. Where we are concerned with the means only, the end being given by others. Here we have only jobs or occupations.

2. Where we may or may not be involved in the formulation of ends (which are given in part by others), but we create the means, which requires skill and training, to fulfill them. Here we are master craftsmen.

3. Where we fully initiate the ends, which are creatively our own inventions and plans, as well as the means to achieve them. Here we are creative artists and our activities are expressed in our careers.

Now it is the latter two kinds of action that are most fulfilling, especially the third, and it is this model that I wish to discuss. For the creatively motivated person there may be so many exciting projects that can be undertaken that often it is difficult to choose between them. Creative endeavors may assume many forms. One may attempt to write a novel, compose a fugue, paint an abstract, draft plans for a monument. Not everyone is capable of these efforts, which entail extremely hard and concentrated effort. Or one can build a patio, form a social club, help to organize a union, run for Congress, create an institution, found a movement. Each of these projects express a person's own interests, and he goes about engaging in instrumental action to realize his goals and ambitions.

Boredom and drudgery can drain us of our motivation and energy. Interesting work can be exuberant and joyful, but only if we envision the possibilities and introduce the means to bring them about. Seminal work is the most meaningful, for it is we who first propound and propose. Granted we need to compose and dispose, and that may require hard and persistent effort; but creative work cannot be abstracted from its initiating purpose. Here there is a harmonious integration of means/ends, efforts/goals, activity/achievement; there is fusion and equilibrium. Both thought and feeling are synchronized with action; process and product are one. It is in those endeavors where we are genuinely interested in the product that we are willing to take infinite pains in what we are doing, have pride in our work, develop an instinct for workmanship, and find it intrinsically rewarding for its own sake, as an end, not simply as a means.

II

There are many purposes that I may have in a lifetime and there are different types of efforts that I may make to fulfill them. Some of my purposes may be short range and limited, such as panelling the den, writing a review, digging a well, completing a course. Some, however, may be long range, such as becoming a surgeon, helping to achieve a stable peace in the world, founding an industry.

Building a career is the best illustration of a long-range aspiration that one may have, for it may take years to achieve. Some critics have denigrated careers and professions, arguing that those involved are engaged in a rat race for success and money and may have lost the capacity to experience values or relate to others. This may be true sometimes; yet the cynics often overlook the great joy in developing a career—work and energy are poured out in order to forge a thing of beauty, a lifework. It is not simply the money or power that motivates people but the sheer excitement of the striving and achieving itself.

Another indictment often made about those who work constantly is that they work so hard that they are unable to enjoy the immediacies of direct experience. They are on the go from morning to night; their life is a hectic maelstrom. There is, of course, often tragic truth in this observation: the frenetic cardiac-prone person is one whose life is full of stress. Yet there also can be a loving relationship to one's work, and the satisfactions of work are often overlooked by the critics. Where life and work are integrated, we can constantly enjoy what we are doing; but work should not blot out other values or make it impossible for us to appreciate others.

We should not, of course, be slaves to our careers. We should not be locked into a profession; we must be willing to change. Hence, increasingly, there is a willingness for the creative person to change careers at midstream, to make new departures, to pick up one's roots and start all over, to be able to enlarge one's horizons.

There is a special quality possessed by the enterprising person. He is not easily satisfied. He can't stand still or rest on his laurels. He is forever trying new things, undertaking new adventures. His is the audacious life of exploration and innovation. Why take a trip, climb a mountain, take on a new task? Because the model for the creative worker is not to sit content and chew his cud, but to move out and do something new. This is the heroic attitude toward work. One can become a leader in one's field, always daring new things and willing to use new methods and techniques. The tried and true of the past should not confine us; we are ready, as adventuresome spirits, to experiment constantly.

As we have seen, this attitude involves courage and

confidence—undertaking something untried is sometimes difficult. There is often high risk and danger. One may lose all. Yet there are challenges that must be met. There is a sense of achievement that goes with all such endeavors. It may be in the form of recognition by others, which is very important. But there is also the matter of self-esteem. Others may or may not approve of what I do or create. But do I approve? Do I like it? Is it a contribution, a job well done? Success is important in this regard—measured by achievement, not necessarily by renown. Did I succeed or fail in what I set out to do? To fail is the test. Not to try for fear of failure is never adequate. If one lacks self-respect, or is excessively shy, or is ineffective as a person, one can only feel miserable.

That is why devotion to work, education, and skill are so important for happiness. To be a craftsman in whatever we do is vital for self-approval. I have found that many college students are overwhelmed by gnawing doubt and worried by the question: What can I do in life and do well? That is what they ask as they try to decide what to major in, what field to enter, what type of career or job to pursue. When they find that they can do something well, they are eager to do it. If, on the contrary, they have a sense that they will fail, life becomes nasty and brutish, full of suffering and tears.

To do creative work one must be receptive to new resonances, but one must also be able and willing to work hard, to exert the effort, to develop the skill to achieve. We need high standards of excellence in our endeavors. Yet it is the give and take between imagination and effort that is at the center of the creative life.

The fullest expression and illustration of creative work is in the area of play, especially games and hobbies. I am not talking about random play, such as that of young children, but about purposeful play; that is, where we play games in order to win, as in competitive sports, or where we play to learn to excel, as in achieving a low golf score or a high bowling score, in learning how to swim well, figure skate, square dance, or ski. All of these activities may be done without a utilitarian purpose. They are forms of relaxation that may indeed be strenous: if we want to achieve something, although it may be fun, it will involve intense practice. Or, too, there are any number of hobbies, like working out jigsaw puzzles, modeling with clay, or learning to play the guitar, that we may undertake. We don't have to do them, but we enjoy them.

We may loathe calisthenics, especially when we are forced, as in an army, commune, or school, to engage in group activities and sports. Yet, if we can do what we freely want to do, we often do not mind the hard physical or psychological effort necessary to complete a task. Parents complain that their children find it difficult to straighten their room or do the dishes, but they have enormous energy to play in the sand or go bike riding.

III

We see, then, that those activities that are freely chosen and that express our own interests and desires are enjoyed best. We particularly thrive on things we do well. We would not necessarily be lazy; we would be energetic and activistic. It's what we are doing and why we do it that counts. But how is it possible, given the conditions of social existence, to find the free time to cultivate autonomous work? Are all individuals capable of such endeavors, or does it really only apply to a creative elite of doers and actors who have the power and money to do what they want? Does not the above model only apply to individuals in the liberal professions, such as law, medicine and teaching, to artists and scientists, to people who are in business for themselves, or to the leaders of industry?

After all, there exists a division of labor and an economic system in which many people have to do what they don't want. Work is generally performed in cooperation with others in organizational units—the factory, office, or groups. Society has the convenient method of rewarding people for loathsome drudgery. They are paid money to do jobs and enter occupations they may not necessarily like.

But, we may ask, can all human work be creative? Or are some people condemned to banal and monotonous jobs? Doesn't someone have to collect the garbage, clean the sewer, and bury the dead? Doesn't someone have to do the menial work, on the assembly lines, in the mines, and on the farms?

A basic question for postindustrial society is, Can we humanize the conditions of labor so that they afford individuals the opportunity for creative, autonomous work? For the first time in human civilization, it seems possible to get rid of, or mitigate, oppressive labor. Human beings may no longer be required to engage in sheer physical toil in order to survive. We now have labor-saving devices and we can produce enough to satisfy our basic needs for food, shelter, and clothing. This, of course, applies largely to affluent societies; as yet, it is far from true in the underdeveloped societies of Asia, Africa, and South America. The point is that we have the technology to free humans from much enforced drudgery. It is not enough to hire people and pay them well; in order to overcome alienation, we need to recreate the conditions of labor itself.

There are a great number of ways that have been recommended to do this. One proposal is that we socialize the means of production. Socialism may be useful in some societies. Yet the problem of alienated labor still has not been solved in the so-called socialist countries, where the state or party has simply replaced the corporation, nor in the public employment sector of capitalist or mixed economies. The average worker is still made to do work that he neither enjoys nor finds creatively rewarding.

Another proposal closely connected to this is to give back to the worker a fairer share of what he earns. For Marx the capitalist allegedly exploits the worker by retaining the worker's surplus labor value in the form of rent, interest, and profit. In a society where there is maldistribution, there is also a wide disparity in degrees of satisfaction. Clearly, some equalitarian considerations, such as progressive income and inheritance taxes, are needed to overcome wide differences in income and wealth. A guaranteed annual minimum wage, social security, unemployment insurance, and other welfare measures help to guard against deprivation.

However, if we believe in providing incentive and rewarding merit, then we should not attempt to achieve a completely egalitarian society or equality of results: this could be counterproductive and oppressive. Even if we were able to achieve a perfect egalitarian society in income and wealth, there might still be substantial differences in the kinds of work that people do—and that is the salient issue. It is not simply a question of giving everyone the same amount of money to buy what they want, but rather of some individuals having more satisfying and creatively inspiring work to do than others.

Still another proposal by B. F. Skinner in *Walden II* would get rid of burdensome and boring occupations per se. Skinner would modify the division of labor. The money system would be replaced by a system of labor credits. Individuals would get more labor credits for doing the shit work than other types of work. Everyone could, if he so chose, do menial jobs to some extent. In China the intellectuals go into the fields to do physical labor. If everyone did some of the physical labor, it would not be a chore but a diversion, and we would willingly do it some of the time. Thus no one would object to cutting the grass, sweeping the cellar, cleaning the toilet. Yet even in *Walden II* there is a class of managers and behavioral scientists, who have more responsibilities than others in running the community. In the last analysis, it is not what you consume, it is what you *do* that counts; and those with the most interesting and influential jobs become members of a new professional elite.

All of these suggestions for reforming work are instructive. Yet I have found that what is perhaps most important in reconstituting work is the need to fuse our means with our ends; that is, wherever possible, to transform labor into a craft, a form of creative activity. This is no doubt difficult in mass industrial or postindustrial societies. But we should realize that we need to involve the worker more in the total process of his work, where he has something to do not only with the means, as labor expended, but with the product or services produced as ends. One way of achieving this is to develop methods of involvement and participation in the total activity of the firm. Participatory democracy allows some sharing of plans and projects. Where workers are simply directed by management, they can easily become mere tools, parts of an organizational structure. Efficiency and productivity are no doubt important considerations, which cannot be dispensed with entirely. Still, involving people in what they do may increase productivity rather than decrease it.

If we could humanize the conditions of labor, work could be more an expression of human purposes. Work is not intrinsically worthwhile for people unless their interests are aroused and they are appreciative of the value of the project. People have to believe that the products or services they are producing are important and that what they are doing is significant. If they do not, their work is likely to be deadening and dull; they are apt to feel that working is more like going to a dentist than making love or going to a ball game or a symphony.

There are, of course, other methods of making work enjoyable. Since the average person spends the best part of his day on the job, the workplace should be made pleasant, wholesome, airy, light. Safety standards and the protection of health must be scrupulously observed. Presumably with increased technology and restricted population growth, it will be possible to minimize the dirty work required by society. People will be able to have more leisure because onerous toil will be reduced. The vocabulary of a preindustrial society no longer needs pertain: we don't have to "work day and night," "put our shoulder to the wheel," or "hand to the plow." Labor-saving devices are replacing strenuous physical efforts: the tractor replaced the ditchdigger, and the electric snake the sewer cleaner. Workers need not be required to put the same nuts and bolts in the same holes on the assembly line year in and year out; their work could have more challenge and variety.

In addition there should be an emphasis on mobility: people should be encouraged, wherever possible, to change their careers at some time. One should not necessarily be a milkman, lawyer, teacher, barber, forger, coal miner, glazier, stone cutter, tanner, potter, coppersmith, hat maker, or wax worker all of his life. Education should be a continuing process, with the universities and colleges open to all age groups in society. One should be able to go back to school for training in another field.

We could do these things if we were to consider work a

creative source of human enrichment, not a form of punishment. Socializing, democratizing, and humanizing the conditions of work can each contribute to this. These are important ingredients in building a fair and equitable economy.

IV

But there is still another essential element that needs to be cultivated. I refer here to the need to develop within each individual an attitude for prizing his work. Undoubtedly our values are conditioned by the social structure; yet it is the individual person and the quality of his motivation that is the basic issue. We should not wait until society solves the problem of alienated labor, but solve it for ourselves. Too many individuals have an ambivalent attitude toward work. Work is a means of getting money to buy the things that they want, including leisure time. Many people dream of "making easy street," where they don't have to do anything. In my view, hell could not be worse.

I grant that our money and exchange system have confused the issue: people are often not rewarded in terms of merit or of what they contribute to the common good, but in terms of the money they can garner. Individuals can make fortunes by speculating in the stock market, winning in a lottery or horse race, or by inheritance; and others can get money by living off of welfare or unemployment compensation. All of these are unearned sources of receiving surplus-value. A just social system would get rid of excessive disproportions of wealth. A leisure group that has contributed nothing may be more lazy than those on the so-called dole. Our consumer-oriented, media-advertising economy has focused on false values of consumption and waste. The good life is drinking beer, smoking cigarettes, using deodorants, spending money, and consuming objects. We have inculcated the wrong values by overemphasizing consumption. It is productive work, not passive consumption, that we need to appreciate. Even in socialist societies, however, similar attitudes toward work often abound. Thus, no matter what the social system, individual attitudes toward work need to be recast. We should not be tied to one job, nor measure its value by what it pays. We are full humans, and our work should express and define our personalities.

The point is that there are positive and rewarding aspects of work aside from its cash-value. Individuals need to discover and appreciate it as a source of joy; it is the active, inventive, creative life that we should seek, not that of the passive consumer, labor drone, or leisure addict. One should ask himself this question: Would you do what you are doing if you weren't paid for it? Or, again, if you were not paid, would you pay society for being permitted to do what you are now doing (assuming that you could afford to)? The most fortunate are those who so love their work that they would do it for nothing, or those who do not wish to retire, because they enjoy their work so thoroughly. On the other hand, the most unfortunate are those who hate their work and wish that they did not have to do what they are doing and would love to quit, if they could. Their whole life is often focused on satisfying consumer wants. They can't wait to retire; many often die soon thereafter for they have nothing productive to do. Yet man is, by nature, a working animal; in one sense this is his differentiating characteristic. We work not simply to consume, but for its own sake. For, unlike all other animals, we invent tools and instruments, change and transform our environment to satisfy new needs and create new interests.

Human culture is grounded in and sustained by work. Without it, life as we know it would not be possible; all of the fruits of civilization would be denied us, including the arts and leisure. Work need not simply have a utilitarian value; it can be aesthetically satisfying in itself.

We can, of course, dream of doing nothing, of basking all day in the sun. Yet life is full of meaning because of what we do and of the projects we are engaged in—and this is true whether they be projects of play and relaxation or of utilitarian service and endeavor. Humans don't have to explore new territories, open up new continents, voyage through the solar system and beyond; yet there is an urgency to do so. That is the Promethean element: to wish to achieve something new, to strain every nerve and muscle, to make something of our lives and our society, to build castles and skyscrapers, to compose works of love and adoration, to discover and create new worlds of visions and ideas. In brief, we exist as doers and creators, not as passive spectators.

Promethean individuals can be audaciously happy; but they are not transcendental meditators cloistered in quiet gardens, but activists—industrious, enterprising, diligent, indefatigable. This elite has invariably discovered some creative work—careers and projects—in which they can pour forth their dreams and express their talents.

Boredom and monotony are the enemies of man—but they are often of our own making. If we wish to banish drudgery from life, then creative work, not God or Utopia, is our salvation. We can become whole and enriched by doing interesting things, as doers and makers. We surely need to satisfy our basic economic needs; the quest for survival is a constant human effort. Beyond that, we can achieve a life of luxury and more: a life energized by creative endeavors for their own sake.

How can one teach a person to express his creative capacities, to work hard and love it, to achieve something and thrill in it? The kingdom of heaven is not the Garden of Eden, where leisure is one's companion. Damnation is doing nothing. Salvation is having a lifework, days over-flowing with zestful activity. Work is not simply working for others, but creating, performing meaningful services, bringing new objects into being. If successful, we can inte-grate effort and play, and unify action and recreation. Such work is intrinsically enjoyable.

The great sin is being lazy and noncreative. The great virtue is fulfilling one's purposes by activity, creating ends that are one's own, and expending the power and energy to achieve them.

Life can be full of gusto and exuberance, but only if one has work to do. Our challenge, if we are to be happy, is twofold: first, in discovering how to make work interesting; second, in learning how to develop interest in some work.

Four / Skepticism versus Gullibility

I

The most important way we have for expressing our powers in the world, resolving ambiguities, and achieving our purposes is by using our critical intelligence. Yet all too often human beings are eager to abandon the use of their reason. The human species has a perverse streak that runs deep in its nature: this is the capacity for being easily deceived; the tendency to allow our wishes, desires, fancies, hopes, or fears to color our imagination or to influence our judgments and beliefs. Confused by false beliefs, many find that happiness eludes their grasp.

Gullibility is the best term to describe this tendency toward self-deception. For humanists, gullibility is the original sin corrupting human nature. It is the willingness to be culled, lulled, or dulled into assenting to a truth claim without adequate evidence or grounds for its support. Gulli-bility is so widely distributed among humans that few are entirely without it. No one can escape its temptation, though there are obviously degrees of perversity or wicked-ness regarding gullibility; but some, by hard therapeutic efforts of will, can cultivate virtue by means of critical intel-ligence. The most gullible sinners in our midst are those who are willing to swallow whole whatever they hear or are promised, to gulp it down—hook, line, and sinker. They are the sitting gulls, ducks, or pigeons—easy prey to every huckster at the fair; they are the suckers, if you will, game for every con man, willing to gobble down everything fed them, unsophisticated, green horns, fall guys. In their most extreme form, they are *Taugenichts* ("good-for-nothings") —pleasant, perhaps charming, yet weak-minded yokels, willingly taken in by the proverbial city slickers.

The problem usually is not so much with the con men —the purveyors of false gods and empty services—who are waiting in the blind for the kill, but in the sitting gulls who are, as it were, pigeonable even to fellow gullibles; that is, they are readily given to self- or co-deception, searching for faith and belief. For the foolables, dupables, stuffables, deludables, hoodwinkables, bamboozlables, hogwashables, humbuggables, born yesterdayables, there seems to be almost a psychological necessity to be taken!

In ordinary life the plain man of common sense can easily spot both the dupes and the con men, and he is able to guard himself against falling prey to their snares and devices. The opposite of the gullible, he is usually the hardnosed skeptic; that is, the person who can smell a rat a mile away, who takes everything with a grain of salt, and who is often difficult to convince. He is usually from Mis-souri, has a look of disbelief when faced with humbug, tends to shrug his shoulders or shake his head, and exclaims, "In a pig's eye!" If he is French, he is likely to roll his eyeballs up and, with a sign of disgust, mutter under his breath, "Merde!" Or if he is from the Bronx, the response he emits is popularly known as a raspberry. The contrast between the gullible and skeptical is one between *instant recall*—repeating what you have been taught—and *instant recoil*—being reluctant to assimilate. Like bitter pills, as Hobbes observed about revealed religion, if swallowed whole they go down easily; but if chewed over, they are instantly spit up.

The skeptical person asks for proof and demands evidence; he tests claims by how well they work out in practice. His antidote for the original sin is critical analysis, which is difficult and demanding, for we are forever prey to temptation. The mind is often weak—how delicious to be gulled into belief. The skeptic is more hoax-proof; but, as I said, skepticism is not easy.

Some people believe that education, a good dose of book learning, is the only cure for gullibility. This is important, but there is no guarantee that it will overcome our innate perversity of wanting to believe. It depends upon the kind of education we are exposed to. Indeed, some of the most cultivated intellectuals are the most easily gulled by the latest fads and fashions. Men of practical wisdom often are less easily gulled than the sophisticated products of the higher learning. There is a kind of native intelligence at work as one goes about the business of living: in finding out why the roof leaks, the drain is stopped up, the car doesn't start.

Generally people are most easily gulled when they are on unfamiliar ground. There they are all too willing to throw caution to the wind and leap in, whereas skeptical persons tread carefully, raising difficult, probing questions. It is especially in fields that require a smattering of learning that gullibility is strongest. Historically, the best illustration is religion, though gullibility is also to be found in science, philosophy, morality, and politics. Nevertheless, religion is notorious because, since it was held sacred, it was immune to critical scrutiny by common sense. There was a great battle between believers and unbelievers—between those who were committed to the orthodox dogmas or received opinions and the heretics, who were not. Each age has its holy gulls, old beliefs deeply ingrained and inculcated generation after generation by authority and tradition as the gospel truth. The gullibles continue to accept the received doctrine on the basis of faith and custom. The skeptic questions its veracity.

Historically the term *freethinker* was used to describe a person skeptical of religious credulity. The freethinker rejected systems of doctrine that rested upon dogma, revelation, custom, or authority. He held that the individual must himself investigate, at least in principle, the claims made and abandon any position whose validity could not be rationally or evidentially demonstrated. In the historic debate a number of epithets, mostly uncomplimentary, have been used by the believers to characterize freethinkers—I should not say debate, because for a long time the orthodox burned freethinkers at the stake. They were the doubters, dissenters, nonconformists, heretics, agnostics, atheists—or more strongly, the infidels, apostates, miscreants, recusants (those who refuse to comply with, or to conform to, religious regulations or practices), nullifidians (persons of no faith or religion), minimifidians (irreligious unbelievers), or just plain backsliders.

At the turn of the century the term *rationalist* was often used interchangeably with freethinker to denote those who attempted to ground religious and other beliefs on reason. More recently the term *humanist* has been used to designate those individuals who are skeptical of religious faith. Humanists generally resist the simple equation of atheism and humanism, for atheism is primarily a negative rejection, whereas the humanist claims to have a more positive ethical philosophy. Whatever else he may be, the humanist is, at root, a skeptic. His natural tendency is to combat gullibility whenever it occurs—though many humanists sometimes are prey in their own philosophies to the same original sin of gullibility as other mortals. Humanists, freethinkers, and rationalists have invariably been skeptical about classical religious theism and have opposed the claims of supernaturalists concerning the existence of God. They are dubious of a whole range of religious beliefs: in biblical miracles and revelation, mysticism and all forms of spiritualism and occultism.

In every age there are people of easy faith who insist that some form of nonsense is absolutely true, ultimately real, and the source of salvation, even though it may transcend the limits of understanding or evidence. Lucian, the Greek philosopher and satirist, described in *Lovers of Lying* how people in the second century A.D. seemed to take pleasure in falsehood for its own sake: quack remedies, charms, miraculous cures, witchcraft, spiritualism, exorcism, expulsion of devils, specters, ghosts, and so forth. He cautioned that the only remedy for such vain and superstitious terms was sound reason and truth. In the sixteenth and seventeenth centuries some of the great scientific minds, such as Kepler and Newton, accompanied their work in astronomy and physics with belief in astrology and biblical revelation. In the nineteenth century William James, Henry Sidgwick, and other philosophers helped to found The Society for Psychical Research whose task it was to investigate psychic phenomena, such as clairvoyance, levitation, the astral body, and survival of the soul—pointing to the prevalence of such beliefs by wide sections of society. Some scientists and philosophers today, dismayed by an epidemic of irrational superstition, wonder if a new Dark Age is about to descend and whether this portends the end of the Enlightenment and the scientific revolution. They are horrified by the great growth of bizzare cults. Thus we are again deluged by a whole range of paranormal beliefs and pseudosciences: demon possession, exorcism, witchcraft, astrology, occultism, scientology, UFO's, chariots of the Gods, telekinesis, levitation, poltergeists, reincarnation, and faith healing. What many fail to see is the near constant presence of such beliefs throughout history. Today we have Billy Graham and a belief in angels, Anton LaVey and the Church of Satan, Jeane Dixon, Uri Geller, and the Maharaj Ji; in the nineteenth century it was Madame Blavatsky and theosophy, the Rosicrucians, Annie Besant, the Reverend Leadbeater, Joseph Smith and the Mormons, to mention only some of the cults.

A cult is a nontraditional religion or rite for the initiated that has not yet been accepted by the establishment. Once it is adopted by a predominant group in society, it becomes an established religion. Most of today's religions were yesterday's cults: they all strain credulity. I am afraid that we most likely will have cults and sects as a permanent part of the social landscape, for they seem to fill a deep psychological need. The only therapy for such perversities of belief is a strong whiff of skepticism.

When I say that one needs, as a corrective, to be committed to reason, I mean it in two ways: first, for judging descriptive, cognitive, or explanatory truth claims; and second—and far more controversial—for making normative or ethical evaluative and prescriptive judgments. Once embodied in one's life and culture, it has an attitudinal effect on the whole person in creating an active disposition.

II

If we should be skeptical about descriptive claims unless they are well-supported, what, may we ask, are adequate grounds for belief? Most assuredly, they are not esoteric or difficult to comprehend. They are indeed similar to those used by the ordinary man in everyday life as he tests the claims of those around him. The scientific method is simply a more sophisticated application of common sense and practical intelligence. I can only sketch what some of its key features are:

First, there is the demand for clear linguistic definitions. If we want to decide whether something is true or false, we need to get rid of confusions caused by vague abstractions. We need to clarify the meaning of the words used. A term or sentence must have some identifiable referent or interpretation based upon human experience, directly or indirectly, if it is to have cognitive significance and meaning. I am not referring to all linguistic terms and sentences but only to those within the context of description; nor am I excluding those items of language that have different functions and uses, such as moral, analytic, expressive, or performatory functions.

Second, there is the bedrock insistence upon evidence —"the damned facts," as they are called—and supporting procedures to test the claim. In order for one to accept a belief, there must be some range of observable data. Here I am referring to an individual's own direct experience, or that of second- or third-hand testimony that is impartially obtained. I surely am not able to check out each occurrence myself; yet if I believe that a sufficient number of reliable observers have done so, I am willing to defer to their judgment. Where the facts are slender or the so-called authorities are special pleaders, one had best suspend judgment. Mere subjective or private appeals that resist any independent confirmation and that cannot be repeated by competent observers must be questioned. The evidence for a belief surely need not be direct—it often is not even in the most advanced theoretical sciences—yet there must be some independent predictive test that will confirm the hypothesis.

Third, there is the criterion of logical validity. We can ask whether the belief is internally consistent, whether it is coherent with other well-founded beliefs that we hold.

Fourth, we also test ideas by how well they serve in practice. Beliefs are judged by whether they help us explain data or resolve problems. To evaluate ideas in pragmatic terms is surely never sufficient in itself. We cannot say simply that ideas without supporting evidence or reasons are true because they are workable. Nevertheless, the pragmatic criterion may be a factor that we consider in a reasoned justification of a belief.

Fifth, where we do not have sufficient supporting data, we ought to suspend or withhold judgment. We should be doubtful of whatever has not been adequately verified. Accordingly, skepticism and agnosticism are important responses for areas in which we do not, as yet, have sufficient evidence. On many topics, then, we should have no opinion until more data are in. That UFO's exist is surely possible; that we were visited by intelligent beings from other planets is possible. Erich Von Daniken's alleged evidence for his thesis, however, is hardly convincing: to accept it we need more conclusive testing.

Sixth, beliefs should be taken as tentative hypotheses, as no more than probable, and open to revision in the light of new evidence—a principle that Charles Peirce labeled "fallibilism." New facts need to be accounted for, and if they cannot, then the theories must be modified. The world view of common sense is often mistaken. We should not be restricted by existing explanations, whether scientific or common sense, of the world. Thus we need to be willing to introduce new theories that go beyond the prevailing perspectives of ordinary life and the sciences. When I refer to common sense, I simply mean that at some point we need to test our hypotheses by hard evidence. Related to this is the need to keep the door open to inquiry. We should be willing to investigate any claim. We should not foreclose future investigation on a priori grounds.

Seventh, we should be receptive to creative imagination, new hypotheses, alternative explanations, fresh departures in thought. Subjective intuition and introspection may be important as the source of novel ideas. However, while they may help to originate ideas, they cannot at the same time validate them. It is one thing to have a glimmer of a new possibility; it is another to maintain that it is therefore true. I reiterate: we continually need to check the authenticity of ideas by independent evidence.

III

There are certain objections that have been raised to the above procedures. Critics maintain that the logical-empirical method is arbitrary, excluding, by definition, whatever cannot meet its antecedent criteria. This closes to us glimpses of the "transcendent" or cuts us off from truths that cannot be known other than subjectively.

I am perplexed by these objections. We should not dogmatically preclude any kind of knowledge. As I have already indicated, we must always leave the door ajar to unsuspected possibilities; we must always be prepared for new dimensions in experience and thought. Surely our knowledge of the universe is meager, given the infinity of events. Surely there are many things that we do not know and that we will uncover in the future. We must not insist that our present world-view or the existing categories of our understanding are final. But when all is said and done, we still have the question of where we go from here. What are the options that are proposed? Which beliefs shall we accept? The only approach to take is the responsible one— let us weigh claims as they are introduced. If someone presents a new belief or theory, a new range of fact, an expanded consciousness, let us examine it carefully. Perhaps he *has* discovered something. But then, we must examine not only his experience or findings but also his *interpretation* and explanation of them and his inferences on the basis of his inquiry. In all such matters I would be at a loss to know *how* to proceed unless the proponent of a new truth is clear about what he means, is coherent and makes sense, and allows us to check his beliefs by reference to our own experience and that of others. We should always be willing to investigate new visions of the universe and pose new questions—but they cannot be accepted as true until they are supported by responsible evidence. That's all that the skeptic, freethinker, and humanist asks of the believer. Is it too much?

Heightened subjective awareness, mystical experiences, and feelings of reverence or awe can be powerful emotional states; we should not seek to denude human life of them. But we should also not delude ourselves about what they mean or point to, if anything, unless and until we can certify or validate their claims. As I have said, there always exists the danger that our perverse tendency to gullibility, will overwhelm us. There are large areas of the unknown and even vast untapped powers that may await further explanation; but again, let us proceed to investigate and explore them, without prematurely announcing what they portend. For example, we should investigate extrasensory perception and paranormal phenomena without drawing premature conclusions on the basis of sketchy evidence as to what they mean about man or the universe.

IV

Thus far we have been discussing descriptive claims about the world and examining how to analyze and appraise their validity. But there is a whole area of life where what is at stake is not what we believe but what we ought to value or do, how we ought to live. Again, there is a tendency to rush in—to follow astrology, to go on a faddist diet, to enroll in an encounter group, to devote one's life to God or country, Marxism, or sexual hedonism.

To what degree can reason intervene? Can objective criteria play a role in warranting value judgments? This area is most complex, for the moral life is full of feeling and passion, impulse and habit.

We surely recognize that there are important uses for reason in ordinary life. Whatever one's values or norms, it is possible to avoid stupid mistakes, foolish or impetuous action, and to use practical reason to control life, moderate desires, mollify passions, and direct actions.

Thus we say that some people are reasonable. They have horse sense, good sense, plain sense, and sound judgment. They manifest prudence and foresight. They are levelheaded, sensible, thoughtful, sagacious, experienced, or deliberate in making choices. On the other hand, gullibility in belief has its counterpart in choice and action. Some people are foolish, irrational, imprudent, impetuous, artless, or inexperienced in their conduct. They manifest a notable lack of wisdom in life. They may bungle and botch, blunder and fumble in their choices. They are, in the extreme, muddleheaded, muttonheaded, thickskulled, fatheaded, boneheaded, noodleheaded, or emptyheaded! These are the people who cannot see an inch before their noses, or who are willing to cut off their noses to spite their faces; they don't have enough sense to come in out of the rain, or they invariably put the cart before the horse, or are penny-wise and pound-foolish, don't know their elbows from holes in the ground (to mix metaphors), are apt to go on wild-goose chases, have too many irons in the fire, play with fire, are willing to buy a pig in a poke, count their chickens before they are hatched; they tend to bark up the wrong tree or to carry coals to Newcastle. They are, if you will, the *nincompoops* of this world! I am afraid that nincompoopery is so widespread that some of my best friends —even though they may be skeptical about descriptive truth claims—often are nincompoops in their personal lives. This especially seems to be a vice of intellectuals.

The opposite of being a nincompoop is attempting to use one's critical intelligence in judging values and making choices, in buying a house, selecting a mate, taking a trip to Florida, or studying for an examination. There is, if you will, a practical logic of decision making that we all recognize. This is analogous, in part at least, to the use of objective intelligence in formulating beliefs about the world. What are its characteristics in outline?

First, practical intelligence seeks to define values, ends, and goals, to understand feelings, wants and needs, to be clear about interests and ideals.

Second, it seeks to ground choices to some extent in a knowledge of the context of action, the circumstances in the situation, the facts of the case. We cannot make intelligent choices unless we know what is at stake, and this includes knowledge of the causal determinants of the present state of affairs.

Third, involved here is a process of deliberation

through which judgments are examined and evaluated, in part by their consistency with other values that we hold.

Fourth, this involves an evaluation of the means at our disposal, the alternatives and available options before us, as well as an appraisal of the probable consequences of various courses of action. In a deliberative process we calculate costs and efficiencies, anticipate likely effects and results, and balance their comparative values. Practical intelligence requires a realistic appraisal of our powers and opportunities, a willingness to engage in creative experiment, and some sense of our limits and constraints.

There is, then, a significant difference between a choice based upon a reflective process of inquiry and one based upon capricious or impulsive reaction—between a reasonable person and a nincompoop. Thus, if I were to name an analogous sin, or perverse streak within our nature, it would be *nincompoopery*. The contrasting humanist virtue is to eat of the fruit of knowledge of good and evil. Alas, nincompoopery, like gullibility, is also widely distributed among human beings who steadfastly avoid moral inquiry. Yet, if we are to lead full lives, lives of autonomy and purpose, we need to resist these snares.

In short, there is no substitute for critical intelligence, both in evaluating truth claims and in deciding how to live. It is the basic tool of life for sensible people. I grant that many people do not wish to be sensible, but I submit that is a constant source of dissatisfaction and failure.

Part II / Enjoyment

Five / Pleasure

I

The autonomous person is not only free to act, fulfilling his own vision of how he wants to live and expressing his own powers in the world, but he also has the capacity to enjoy life deeply. Thus concomitant with the strenuous mood is the need to develop an appreciation for the immediacies of experience. The full life, while it involves the outgoing activation of our talents, also includes the ability to savor delicious experiences for their own sake. We can't work all the time; we need relaxation, play, enjoyment.

There are many individuals who are unwilling to try new things or to extend the range of their enjoyments. Yet it is diversity that adds zest to the fullness of life. For some individuals any self-indulgence in pleasure is wrong. Afraid to let themselves go, they go through life denying themselves new experiences and tastes. Their emotional life is dammed up and repressed, their souls dried up and dwarfed; they are closed to the farthest reaches of human enjoyment.

This fear of pleasure may be labeled *hedonic-phobia*. In extreme cases it is morbid and pathological. Typically, the hedonic-phobic may be celibate, may never, or rarely ever, drink, he labors hard, may lead a sheltered existence, or he may conform to social conventions and confine his pleasures to the culturally acceptable. The hedonic-phobic, for example, may have a limited diet. When he is at a restaurant he invariably orders the same thing from the menu—only what he knows he likes. He is unwilling and unable to try new foods: he disdains snails, steak au poivre, chèvre, or bouillabaisse. If he drinks, he generally selects the same drink each time: sherry, martini, or scotch on the rocks; he is reluctant to try a slinger, Moscow Mule, grasshopper, or Alexander. His sexual passions are generally narrow, and though he may fantasize about a wide range of sexual delights, God forbid that he should ever indulge his wishes! Sexual adventure is distasteful to him.

Hedonic enjoyment is, or should be, an essential ingredient in the good life. This does not mean that pleasure is the only good; nor should we live only to experience pleasurable sensations. Another malady of the soul, the opposite of hedonic-phobia, but equally destructive, is *hyperhedonism*: a life devoted largely to the quest for hedonic thrills. This type of life is self-defeating. It is commonly found in youthful persons who, for example, in first discovering the excitement of sex, drink, or drugs, become enamoured of their thrills, to the exclusion of all else. Some individuals never go beyond that, and their lives, being devoted to pleasures alone, become banal.

The classical hedonists were mistaken in their theory of human nature when they claimed that the pleasure-pain principle is the sole spring of human motivation. For it is not pleasures by themselves in abstraction from the underlying life-activities that we seek, but the pleasures comingled with activity and experience. If I am thirsty and quench my thirst with a glass of refreshing iced tea, it is the drinking of the tea that I like, not simply the pleasure by itself. If I enjoy a good steak, it is whiffing its tempting aroma, biting into and chewing its succulent meat that I relish, not the pleasure in isolation. Pleasures always appear in a context of life-action: they are not abstract sensuous forms. The error of hedonism as a theory is that it is based on a speculative psychological thesis that reifies sense experience distinct from objects and interests.

Nevertheless, if pleasure is not in itself the end, it is intimately interwoven with our goals, adding qualities and tones, vivifying and enhancing them. To be able to find pleasure in various activities and experiences is to expand our horizons and to add an important dimension to life. The kind of hedonism that I would defend is *robust hedonism;* that is, deriving pleasure from a wide range of experiences, activities, persons, and things. In order to enjoy widely, we must be receptive to the assorted flavors of life. We should be prepared to expand the parameters of our experience—intellectual, cognitive, perceptual, motivational. If our experiences are diverse, our life is more apt to be interesting. We are defined by what we do, by the objects of our desire and thought, by how and what we experience. If our experiences are narrow, we are narrow as human beings. Some persons are limited in their options, choices, and experiences. One who spends his entire life confined by the existing boundaries of his social world is condemned to a humdrum existence.

There is a stage in life when one must be prepared to break out into the broader world and experience a medley of enjoyments. It is not simply pleasure that should be the rudder of life, but the richness and variety of experienced

activities. One needs to cultivate an attitude of openness.
This again involves risks: it involves receptivity to discovery.
We need to venture forth and to take chances, to be curious
about new windows that we can open. We should be able to
enjoy pleasures lustily and mightily.

II

Are all pleasures good? Is there any standard for
judging their worth? Are some better than others, some
"noble," others "demeaning"?

Philosophers and theologians have long debated this
issue, and there has been an unfortunate effort, from Plato
to Mill, to make a sharp distinction between the so-called
"higher" and "lower" pleasures. Typically the "lower"
pleasures were held to be biological, and involved the pleasures of food, drink, sex, and touch; the "higher" pleasures
were said to be spiritual, intellectual, moral, and aesthetic.
Jeremy Bentham refused to make a distinction and said
that pushpin was as good as poetry.[1] According to Bentham, if we were to measure pleasures by a hedonic calculus,—by their intensity and purity, for example—we might
find little quantitative difference. Mill argued that pleasures
need to be judged qualitatively, not simply quantitatively,
and that they differed in kind: "It is better to be a human
being dissatisfied than a pig satisfied; better to be Socrates
dissatisfied than a fool satisfied."[2]

In a sense both Bentham and Mill were correct: a pleasurable experience, taken in itself, is good, not evil. However, there are differences in qualitative feelings and in the
kinds of pleasure we experience, and we cannot simply
measure all pleasures on the same scale. The pleasure of a

1. Jeremy Bentham. "An Introduction to the Principles of Morals and Leg-
islation" in *The Utilitarians* (New York: Doubleday, 1973).
2. J. S. Mill, *Utilitarianism*, op. cit., page 410.

kiss is not the same as that of a sonata, nor is that of a poem the same as that of a rose.

It is a mistake, however, to divide our experiences into "higher" and "lower" and to condemn the latter as being of lesser value, as some moralists have done. This masks a destructive prejudice against the body and a bias of the so-called educated taste against the simple pleasures of the ordinary person. One may say that, although pleasure in and by itself is good, it is the relationship of pleasure to conduct and to other aspects of our experience that may sometimes make it undesirable.

Are there criteria for judging pleasures on a scale of values? Yes, and we discover them in living. In the first case, as I have already pointed out, one who lives exclusively for pleasures, measuring every deed by its hedonic tone, is ego-centered, perhaps even autistic. We learn in life that we need to weigh our pleasures in the contexts of various activities. We judge them by whether or not they are appropriate to situations or whether they are out of place. A child seeks self-gratification and is unaware of the conditions or consequences of his action. A mature adult has some measure for self-control, for he evaluates pleasures by their cost and results. Many pleasures that we seek are not worth the price that we have to pay, in money and reputation, if nothing else. Thus we learn to balance our pleasures. We make plans and projects, and we calculate the expenditures needed to achieve them; and we may decide that the realization may not measure up to the effort. Intelligence intervenes. A rational person soon learns that some pleasures, however enticing, require too great a sacrifice, and that the consummation may not be as great as the anticipation.

Maturity teaches that some moderation in certain kinds of pleasure is advisable. We can go overboard in emphasizing one kind of pleasure to the exclusion of others:

a dope eater, alcoholic, or sexually promiscuous person can obliterate other types of enjoyment. Character develops self-restraint. This need not be the same thing as the super-ego, imposed by society, the church, or the law; nor need it be based upon edicts against forbidden fruit, full of "thou shalt nots." There is a kind of inner discipline of practical intelligence. We learn, for example, that too much whiskey can lead to the morning hangover and to cirrhosis of the liver, that indiscriminate one night stands can lead to crabs and clap, or that a gourmet's extravagance can cause gallbladder trouble. Some pleasures, if taken in excess, can be positively debilitating. Only a fool will risk all for a few moments of pleasure. There is a wisdom of the body that can guide and restrain our appetites. We learn that hell hath no tyranny like a craving gone wild. One is forever tormented and given no respite; a passion inordinately unleashed can make equanimity impossible.

Thus there is a criterion that the philosophers have recognized: the role of reason in moderating passion. But we should be clear that there is a vast difference between reason that is censorious and condemnatory and reason that is selective and cultivating. The former, if excessive, says no to pleasure. The latter says yes, pleasures of course, but in moderation and with balance. Reason thus functions to ensure the body's health.

Still another important way to evaluate pleasure is in relation to our basic needs. The human organism has a set of primary biological needs that require satisfaction, if one is to be healthy and vigorous. Hedonic-phobics often are repressed in regard to one or more basic needs. Thus one cannot genuinely experience many kinds of feelings and emotions if one is blocked in certain basic drives. We have many basic needs: homeostatic and growth needs related to proper nutrition and health, sexual needs, the need for love, the need to belong to some community, the need for self-respect, and so forth. Abraham H. Maslow and others have pointed to a hierarchy of needs in the human person. If the basic needs are not satisfied, we may be profoundly morose, in a state of anxiety and tension, unable to function fully or to relish life.

This points directly to the importance of growth; there is a continuum of development through which a person comes to learn and appreciate new things. There are powerful latent forces that can be realized. Many of these are subtle and complex—such as a full appreciation for sexuality, the development of one's intellectual abilities and aesthetic sensitivities, or the growth of moral awareness. There are a whole range of tastes that need to be cultivated. To appreciate them we may need to work at it. Living involves constant learning. We can become connoisseurs of fine wines and delicacies, art and poetry, science and philosophy. We go through stages of moral growth, and at some point we develop cognitive moral awareness instead of blind obedience to a moral code.

The key ingredients here are a capacity for actualization and the willingness to expand and unfold. It is not simply expressing an inner nature or being; nor is it discovering something within myself that I simply give vent to. This is surely involved in growth. Yet many of the richest sources of pleasure are not achieved by realizing our nature —though it is necessary that we do this. To "know thyself" and act accordingly is not enough. Growth implies creativity and this means that we need to *out*grow ourselves, not be hemmed in or determined by urges beyond our control. It means, in one sense, that I must *exceed* my nature, redefine and recreate it. For the human universe is an invented world: it is not given per se, but taken and transformed. It is the transforming character of human choice that opens up the possibilities for new kinds of pleasure. What is music but a human invention? Strings played in unison with horns, reeds, and percussion instruments become a symphony, which can be transformed into a stereophonic recording that can be listened to continually and enjoyed for its own sake. One cannot claim that we are made by nature to appreciate stereophonic music, for it is a new world that we have created from which we derive inspiration. That humans were made to achieve the joys of floating in spaceships is surely nonsense; we have been limited by millions of years of evolution to adapt to the force of gravity on earth. But we can find the experience of space travel intensely enjoyable and euphoric.

Thus human growth can be ever-expanding. We are not limited to fulfilling what we are intrinsically, but can *become* what we want; and we can find great excitement in the act of becoming. We can become many things and we can move in many different directions. There are seemingly infinite varieties and open possibilities for development. What directions will we take? What shall we choose to invent? What new forms of enrichment will we create?

What are essential here are curiosity, ingenuity, innovation. Our world is full of objects and events that give us pleasure because we have cultivated new tastes and interests.

The hyperhedonist all too often is fixated only on limited pleasures: he lacks the spirit of adventure, discovery, invention. He lacks the creative spark. But pleasure and creativity go together; and creativity adds zest and vitality to existence. There is no creativity without intelligence and a desire to learn new things; nor without courage, audacity, a willingness to dare, and to break new ground. These are all pleasures related to human power and achievement.

We come back, however, to an earlier question. Do some people, given the conditions of modern society, lack the means to find enjoyment? Have the division of labor, the monetary system, and the distribution of power prevented full growth, enjoyment, intelligence, and creativity for them? To argue in such terms and to blame the environment is to confess one's own limitations as a person. One must recognize that there can be extreme deprivation. Granted also that money and power are useful and that there are minimal resources that we need (though these are relative, not absolute, standards). But the creative life is an expression of personal attitude no matter what the social conditions; and the capacity to live the full life is a dynamic that can be tapped from within.

One might say, it does not cost much money to write a letter, go swimming, sing a song, go to a museum, walk in the park, enjoy a tulip, drink in the sky, kiss a lover, play with a puppy, read a good book, climb a mountain, enter a race, write haiku, hold hands with a friend, plant orchids, swim in a cool lake, roast chestnuts, deliver a speech, spend an afternoon at an art gallery, watch a hockey game, listen to Bartók, engage in conversation, prepare a soufflé, whittle a statue, read early-Marx, fight for a cause, crack a joke, sing in a chorus, hum a tune, or play the harmonica! Those who bemoan their incapacity to enjoy are engaging in a form of self-deception. For if a person lacks creativity, all the money or power in the world cannot purchase it, nor give one happiness if he or she is empty. Although external conditions are relevant and can hinder or help our projects, the state of our mood and our purposes depends, in the last analysis, upon the person *himself.* It depends on one's own imagination and receptivity.

III

In spite of numerous opportunities for enjoyable experiences in life, many persons find life boring, dull, monotonous, wearisome. There are degrees of boredom. The bored person may have a negative and pessimistic outlook on life. In an extreme form, such a person is overwhelmed by depression, unable to sleep, full of anxiety and tension, repressed and fearful. Many people, although not psychic-depressive per se, are nevertheless troubled with boredom. Psychologist Sol Gordon, believes that boredom is epidemic in our time. It infects all age groups and classes —the young, adolescents, students in college, workers on the job, the wealthy and the poor, and older persons. It has numerous symptoms. People who have it often hate to get up in the morning; they dread facing the day. They are easily tired or often fall into a state of lassitude. They inevitably complain that "there is nothing to do," "no place to go," no way "to pass the time." The bored person doesn't like to be alone for fear of ennui. Yet he blames other people for his being bored, or he blames his surroundings for his boredom (especially if he lives in a place like Indianapolis, Scranton, or San José). He hates his job or the school he goes to, or his wife or colleagues.

The hedonic-phobic often finds life boring—and no wonder, since it is denuded of pleasure. There are few thrills that he will dare to discover. He is closed to life. But, at the other extreme, the hyperhedonist is likewise easily bored. If one lives only for immediate pleasures, the pursuit of them can be maddening, and one may need ever bigger and better forms of titillation to keep one interested. The hyperhedonist condemns himself to a vacuous and trivial life. He lacks a lifework or creative endeavors to fascinate him; he is adolescent in his craving for pleasurable satisfaction. He is not self-stimulated but needs to be stimulated by others.

The person who says he is easily bored is revealing his own inadequacies: he is really confessing that he is boring to be with, he is small-minded and emotionally underdeveloped, of limited tastes and horizons. He is not fully alive. If he is boring, it is inevitable that he will surround himself with other bores.

The opposite of boredom is vitality: the creative hedonist can't sit still a minute, he doesn't know the meaning of boredom. Life is exciting, invigorating, full of opportunity and interest. He feels that there are not enough hours in the day to do all the things that he wants to do. Many projects and plans compete in their appeal. His outlook is inwardly positive and optimistic. He exudes confidence, exuberance, gusto (which, incidentally, bores the boring person).

How does one combat boredom? people often ask. How does one live fully? I reply! The fact that someone is easily bored is puzzling, given the boundless opportunities for enjoyable experiences afforded by modern society. The marvelous things that we can do are far beyond the range of previous societies. The average person today can enjoy luxuries that formerly were the preserves of privileged aristocracies, and these involve the whole gamut of life experiences. Perhaps some of these should be enumerated, for the bad things are constantly pointed out by the prophets of gloom, and the bountiful joys are all too often overlooked.

IV

[*Note: If the reader finds the following section boring, he may move on to the next. It is a brief catalogue of only some of the pleasures that can be discovered.*]

The entire world, and all it offers, has now become our vista. It includes the totality of human culture and history: from the aboriginal society of Australia, the mandarin civilization of China, the sophisticated cultures of London,

Amsterdam, New Delhi, and Tokyo, to the alpine wonders of Switzerland, the warm beaches of the Carribean, the oases of the Middle East, and the jungles of Brazil. We can travel and enjoy these regions and cultures, or at least import products from all parts of the globe; gourmet delicacies abound.

We can consume Chateaubriand, corned beef and cabbage, Boston baked beans, chili con carne, lobsters, squid, trout, fish and chips, bacon and eggs, bagels and lox, Borscht, chop suey, lasagna, tamale, kidney pie, and casseroles made with sauce à la russe, à la suisse, à l'espagnole, à la bordelaise, à la bearnaise, à la lyonnaise, à la milanaise, au gras, au gratin, au jus, au kirsch, and au vin blanc!

Among the succulent vegetables to choose from are shallot; summer squash; escarole; lima beans; corn on the cob; zucchini; Brussel sprouts; Bermuda onions; asparagus; artichokes; french fried, Idaho, and sweet potatoes; and salads—green, tossed, Waldorf, coleslaw, fruit, and julienne.

We can season our food with chive, garlic, radish, pimento, horseradish, ginger, chutney, clove, marjoram, savory, salt, sage, mayonnaise, mustard, paprika, nutmeg, parsley, red pepper, vanilla, tabasco, tartar, and thyme.

For dessert we can savor éclairs and cream puffs, lemon meringue pie, chocolate cake, strawberry shortcake, cheese cake, crème caramel, mousse au chocolate, and crème de maron.

We can drink orange juice, lemonade, cranapple, beer, soda, malted milk, coca cola, ambrosia, buttermilk, chicory, frappé, nectar, phosphate, chocolate cream, sarsaparilla, café espresso, tea, cocoa, or Turkish coffee.

Fruit dishes include guava, loganberry, grapes, Catawba, citrus, melons, pineapple, currant, pomegranate, sugarplum, figs, watermelon, kumquat, and papaya.

The cheese platter is full: Bel Paese, bleu, Camembert, Port Salut, Gorgonzola, Parmesan, Munster, Roquefort, Provolone, Liederkranz, Neufchatel, Romano, Swiss, New York, Wisconsin, Tilsiter, cheddar, edam, ricotta, gouda, or gruyère.

The nut bowl includes chestnuts, almonds, cumara nuts, filberts, hazelnuts, walnuts, pecans, pistachios, and cashews.

And there are bon bons galore: butterscotch, caramel, peanut brittle, peppermint, licorice, fudge, marshmallow, chocolate, Suchard, Hershey, marzipan, mint, halavah, horehound, taffy, toffee, or tutti-frutti.

And we can enliven our eating with Bourdeaux, Burgandy, scotch, bourbon, Liebfraumilch, Chablis, Chianti, Moselle, Riesling, Madeira, May wine, Malaga, vermouth, champagne, tequila, saki, bitters, cognac, rum, gin, vodka, rye, Benedictine, Grand Marnier, anisette, Drambuie, curacao, or kümmel.

We can adorn our apartments, homes, villas, haciendas, shacks, or caves with flowers: poinsettias, violets, azaleas, chrysanthemums, lilacs, lilies of the valley, marigolds, mayflowers, pansies, roses, Queen Anne's lace, primrose, rosemary, sage, orchids, morning-glory, fuchsia, carnations, begonias, asters, Chinese lanterns, dahlias, daisies, and dandelions.

For clothing we can wear cashmere, nylon, tweed, gaberdine, flannel, wool, lace, silk, blazers, pinafores, sarongs, Mackinaws, jerkins, frock coats, Levis, tuxedos, ski pants, toreador pants, denims, cordoroys, blue jeans, Bermuda shorts, bell bottoms, culottes, evening gowns, hoop skirts, jumpers, bathrobes, kimonos, B.V.D.'s, fedoras, bonnets, top hats, turbans, anklets, mittens, ascot ties, Chesterfields, kerchiefs, French cuffs, girdles, scarves, Oxfords, moccasins, bootees, or T-shirts.

It is not only the world of delicacies and luxuries that we have to consume; the opportunity for new delights, aesthetic and mental, are also multifarious. We can see a variety of plays and movies, learn to appreciate and enjoy the arts. And we can engage in the discovery of new ideas and concepts, new books and theories, new attitudes and values. We can, by the written word, experience in cognition and imagination new worlds that we have not yet seen or conquered.

We can appreciate the world of music of Beethoven, Brahms, Bach, Mozart, Tschaikovksy, Wagner, Debussy, Hindemith, Bartók, Stravinsky, Copeland.

We can enjoy boleros, minuets, nocturnes, polkas, scherzos, spirituals, serenades, elegies, fugues, sonatas, jigs, waltzes, toccatas, operas, or jazz, bebop, acid rock, the Beatles, Rolling Stones, Elton John, Joan Baez, Louis Armstrong, and Mahalia Jackson.

There is the piano, violin, clarinet, oboe, banjo, mandolin, cello, bass, saxophone, harpsichord, trombone, bassoon, bagpipes, balalaikas, accordion, organ, clavichord, hurdy-gurdy, glockenspiel, marimba, xylophone, castanets, drums, tom-tom, or tambourine.

We can enjoy various styles of art: classical, abstract, traditionalist, representational, baroque, gothic, cubist, dadaist, expressionist, romantic; Da Vinci, Brach, Miro, Calder, Matisse, Brancusi, or Warhol.

We can take up architecture, sculpture, photography, drawing, portrait painting, ceramics, pottery.

Or we can read the poets: Wordsworth, Whitman, Simonides, Sandburg, Shelly, Ginsberg, Keats, Milton, Goethe. And the dramatists: Euripides, Shakespeare, Ibsen, Shaw, O'Neil, Albee, Brecht. And the novelists: Fielding, Austin, Dickens, Flaubert, Faulkner, Mann, Dostoyevsky, Solzhenitsyn, Hemingway, and Bellow.

We can read about science fiction, astrology, astronomy, theology, Zen Buddhism, and the mystic cults.

We can investigate the sciences: physics, biology, psychology, physiology, chemistry, sociology, cybernetics, anthropology, political science, history, archeology, geology, economics, and linguistics.

Or we can learn the skills of the medical arts: dentistry, chiropody, osteopathy, hemopathology, neurology, gynecology, psychiatry, or nosology.

There is an infinite variety of goods that civilization and nature have offered humans to be experienced and enjoyed: boats, cars, bicycles, airplanes, dirigibles, skates, sleds, schools, monasteries, cathedrals, temples, canyons, volcanoes, rivers, lakes, oceans, trees, plants, rocks, furniture, tools, toys, and games. The list is endless!

V

It should be abundantly clear that any effort to make a sharp distinction between the "higher" and "lower" pleasures is doomed to failure. Rather we want as many types of pleasure as possible: physical, intellectual, moral, aesthetic, and spiritual. To emphasize only some kinds of pleasure to the exclusion of others is to narrow one's options.

However, if we are to be able to appreciate fully, we need to develop some basic personality characteristics: we must be willing to try new things and taste new experiences. The robust hedonist says, "Taste it, you'll like it," and the hedonic-phobic says, "No, I'd better not, I might not like it." But we must be prepared to seek out new experiences in life, to take risks, to seize opportunities, to respond to challenges. We must venture forth, without fear or guilt. Courage and power are the keys to a wide range of new pleasures and activities. The main thing is to pursue activities that we like; pleasures will follow to enhance and complete them.

Related to this is the need to grow in our capacities and interests. We must develop a full appreciation for intellectual and aesthetic activities. We need to continuously keep alive our sense of curiosity and wonder. Education and learning should never cease. There are always new things to uncover, new forms of knowledge, new ideas to intrigue us, new intellectual and experiential adventures.

The creative outlook, as we have seen, involves a life-work, a sense of one's own power and worth as a human being. To find life fulfilling, one must be able to pursue one's own private purposes. But happiness also involves—distinctively—the ability to share experiences with other persons: to love and be loved. This means that we are also receptive to the delights of erotica.

Six / Eroticism

I

A vital ingredient of the full life is the ability to enjoy pleasures that are erotic, to find delight in the sensual, to be aroused by beauty, to be allured by the caress of touch, to savor the sensuous form, the fragrance and romance of sexuality and love. Although the good life involves the active mood, the strenuous attitude of exertion and achievement, it also involves some rest and repose, the ability to capture the moments of tender feeling and enraptured ecstasy. Not to suffer the pangs of passion or be moved by their fervor and attraction is not to have lived fully; without passion, life would be lacking something poignant. The erotic thus plays a significant role in the full life. Yet, there are the disciples of virtue who consider the main problems in life to be the control or extirpation of the erotic. *Erotic-phobia* is only one aspect of a broader *hedonic-phobia*, or distaste for pleasure. It has deep cultural roots, particularly in the West.

The classical view of happiness of the philosophers—
Plato, Aristotle, Spinoza, Bentham, Mill—has generally
tended to minimize the importance of sexual desire. Reason's main task was to control the passions or moderate
them by means of temperance. For Plato, the chariot of the
soul was drawn by three horsemen—reason, appetite, and
ambition—and the task of reason was to order the other two
so that they might all move in the same direction. The
philosophers were not necessarily against the erotic per se,
but they thought that anyone devoted to it could be driven
mad by its allure. The life of pleasure was like a leaking
pitcher, argued Plato; it could never be filled. One may
grant that some temperance is essential if one is to lead a
full life, and that reason has an important moderating function to perform. But in the philosophical literature we rarely
find an appreciation for the positive dimensions of erotic
sexuality.

It is in the Judeo-Christian religious tradition, especially exemplified by Paul, Augustine, and Calvin, that one
finds the clearest cases of erotic-phobia; in each there is an
explicit effort to suppress sexuality as "wicked" and a morbid detestation of the erotic—which was supposed to be
replaced by *agapé*, or spiritual love. Paul condemned the
pleasures of the flesh, including "adultery, fornication,
uncleanliness, and lasciviousness."[1] Augustine gave vent to
a central moral bias of Christianity when he admonished
that "the flesh should cease to lust against the spirit, and
. . . there [should] be no vice in us against which the spirit
may lust."[2] Instead, asceticism and celibacy were heralded
as moral virtues. In his *Confessions*, Augustine railed
against the "diseases of the soul," and he asked for deliv-

1. *Galatians* 5: 19-20.
2. *The City of God*, Bk. XIX, pp. 303-4 (New York: Hafner Publishing Co.,
1948), Vol. II.

erance from "vile affections," especially the sexual passions. Being a "slave to lust," he thought, was shameful and sinful. One could only be redeemed by God by abandoning the temptations of the erotic.

The denigration of the body and of sexual acts continued in the Church. It is illustrated, for example, by Lotario dé Conti, who became Pope Innocent III in the twelfth century:

> How filthy the father; how low the mother; how repulsive the sister. . . . Dead human beings give birth to flies and worms; alive, they generate worms and lice. . . . Consider the plants, consider the trees. They bring forth flowers and leaves and fruits. But what do *you* bring forth? Nits, lice, vermin. Trees and palms exude oil, wine, balm—and *you*, spittle, snot, urine, ordure. *They* diffuse the sweetness of all fragrance—*you*, the most abominable stink. . . . We who shrink from touching, even with the tips of our fingers, a glob of phlegm or a lump of dung, how is it that we crave for the embraces of this mere bag of night-soil? . . . (God has decreed that) the mother shall conceive in the stink and nastiness.[3]

Morbid taboos against sexuality follow from this aversion. Erotic-phobia is a pathological state of mind. In its excessive form, as asceticism and celibacy, it is unhealthy, denying the individual the nourishment necessary for the quickening of life. The fear of eroticism has deep roots within our culture; sex was considered by many to be obscene, lewd, salacious, prurient, lascivious, concupiscent.

The modern world has had to struggle to be liberated from the phobic view of sex. Nietzsche attacked the sins that the Church had committed against the body and called for a new set of values. Freud bade us to gain an apprecia-

3. Aldous Huxley, "Hyperion to a Satyr," in *Tomorrow and Tomorrow and Tomorrow* (New York: Harper, 1956), pp. 151-53.

tion for the role of our unconscious drives, and he pointed to the need to release the libido from excessive repression. And Marcuse recognized the tendency of civilization to repress eros and the polymorphous perverse and pointed out all the pathological symptoms that result from doing so.

The release of our erotic tendencies and our ability to appreciate sexual pleasure is essential if we are to achieve the good life. The failure of classical philosophy was that it ignored or undervalued sexuality. The destructive character of authoritarian religion was in its seeking to repress and extinguish sexuality. But we need to cherish and cultivate sex, for it helps to open for us the portals of happiness.

II

Eroticism has many dimensions. It arouses within us an appreciation for love. *Eros,* son of Aphrodite, was the god of love; and the *erotic* is related to romantic affection. But it also focuses on the stimulation of the genitalia and the pleasures of sexual arousal, and it culminates in orgasm. Beginning with sexual intercourse, it leads to an appreciation of a wide range of sexual tastes and passions—from the kiss and touch to fondling, caressing, and other forms of erotic stimulation. This latter sense seems to be basic. The erotic can be diffused; it can assume a variety of expressions. Having its roots in sexual acts, it may be elaborated with subtlety and delicacy. Being open to the erotic is to enter a new world of *aesthetic-hedonic* appreciation: the capacity for discovering the pleasures of the sensuous as they are revealed in ourselves and others. To be closed to those pleasures is to be blind to the richness of life.

It is important that we focus first on the generalized erotic as distinguished from love or sex per se, for there are those who would criticize the erotic if it is isolated from some loving relationship; or, on the other hand, who would relate the erotic in every case to sexuality. One can have sex where there is little or no love present: here sex is no more than a release from an itching in the genitalia. Similarly, loving affection has many dimensions, such as that of parents for children or of friends for each other. The relationship between lovers is deeply sexual, but it may involve other interests and concerns: the sharing of plans and dreams, living and working together, building a home or a family.

Thus the erotic per se cannot be identified solely with either sex or love. The erotic, no doubt, has its roots in sex and its highest fulfillment is in romantic love; but it is limited or thwarted, in my judgment, unless it can be intimately diffused with a whole variety of human experiences. The erotic is related to sensory stimulation in a most fundamental way. There is a good deal of psychobiological evidence that humans and other primates need sensory or tactile sensations, if they are to develop normally.

Thus, infants love to be picked up and handled, not only to be fed and cleaned, but to be stroked and rocked. The infant cries when it is hungry or is in pain, and it instinctively begins sucking the breast or bottle nipple at birth. Unless an infant is able to satisfy its biological needs, it will not survive or grow normally. Not only does the child need food, drink, and protection, but it needs to feel the warmth and affection of mothering care by another, whether a real or surrogate parent.

There is dramatic evidence that children who lack such direct contact—squeezing, cuddling, fondling, hugging, kissing—do not develop normally or emotionally. Continued deprivation assaults the very being of the emerging human person, who may languish and wither. This is not unique to humans: monkeys demonstrate similar needs, puppies show pleasure when petted, and kittens purr.

In a sense, being able to respond to touch is related to one's erotic life. Sexuality does not begin simply at puberty but is deeply expressed in the infant, child, and preadolescent throughout all stages of development. The hunger for touch is something that never leaves us entirely: to touch and be touched, to feel hands and bodies, and to kiss, hug, and caress satisfy a deep craving within.

Children who are deprived tend to develop pathological manifestations, from autism to failure to relate to others. James W. Prescott has shown that the seeds of violence are found in sensory deprivation.[4] Inability to relate affectionately as an adult often triggers aggression, hostility, and violence.

Some deprived adults have an aversion to being touched: the body becomes stiff, any physical contact leads to an inflexible skeletal reaction. Such persons may or may not be capable of sexual orgasm: they find it difficult to fondle or be fondled, to caress and enjoy contact with another's flesh. They seem to be imprisoned by their own rigidities. The encounter movement and the new psychotherapies are an effort to reawaken a receptivity to touch and to open up individuals so that they can naturally enjoy their own bodies.

This erotic stimulation is diffused over the whole body of the infant. Those adults who have enjoyed a "trip around the world," that is, generalized sensuous stimulation from head to toe, know that it is not simply the penis, vagina, breasts, anus, or lips that are pleasure centers, but that the entire body can become an erogenous zone.

The erotic development of a person continues throughout life. It is essential that young children have recurring affection from parents and playmates. They constantly need physical affection; games of exercise keep youngsters in touch with each other.

One of the great traumas of adolescence occurs at pu-

4. See "Before Ethics and Morality," *The Humanist* (Nov./Dec., 1972); "Abortion and the Unwanted Child," *The Humanist* (March/April, 1975).

berty, when there is an awakening of new capacities and desires. The young girl is able to menstruate and the young boy to ejaculate. The first exploration may begin with self-examination. The adolescent discovers that his or her own body is a source of gratification and pleasure, as he or she may have wet dreams and learn to masturbate.

It is tragic when one's natural sexual expression becomes suppressed by social taboos. In some societies—including our own—masturbation has been held to be sinful. Young people have been warned that masturbation could lead to perversion and insanity and that premarital intercourse could lead to incurable disease. What is the growing adolescent to do when his or her vital sexual powers, which emerge full-blown at age twelve or thirteen, are supposed to be suppressed and held in abeyance until marriage at eighteen or nineteen, or even later. No wonder that sex-starved and love-hungry adolescents often are traumatized by life. It is as if we were to tell a child: thou shalt not defecate, because it is wicked; neither shalt thou clap thy hands with pleasure nor jump for joy, for to do so is to commit a mortal sin. Fortunately, in recent years a more sensible attitude toward adolescent sexuality, has been developing—though many parents and educators still consider it wrong for adolescents or postadolescents to "have sex." They are unaware that to keep sexual desires bottled up may lead to more problems than it prevents. Now that the two great fears of adolescent sex can be obviated— we can prevent pregnancy with contraceptives and can cure venereal disease with antibiotics—the normal expressions of human feelings and erotic stimulation in the growing process should be permitted. Puppy love is among the most beautiful of human experiences and should be nourished, not condemned.

Every stage of life has its erotic needs and desires, old age as well as youth. Just as our culture has condemned infant and adolescent sexuality, it has done likewise with senescent sexuality. Yet, sexual passion and the need for affection and love are never fully extinguished. Therefore it is important that they be satisfied as long as a person is able to satisfy them. One of the key signs of vigor in old age is an interest in erotic activity. A life is incomplete if we cannot tingle with feelings, light up with sexual interest, palpitate with desire, or be sensitive to the touch of another. Part of the enchantment of life is our capacity to feel wanted, to relate to and enjoy the good things of life with another, to be awakened by romance, to rekindle old passions. Life can be a wondrous delight for those who can thrill and throb to another: the holding of hands, the fond caress, the kiss of endearment, and the feelings of sexual potency. Thus we should never shut off the erotic, for it heightens and makes possible the fullness of life.

There are substitutes for direct sensual touch, and these are especially related to the eye. So-called pornographic literature and art is able to arouse erotic sensibilities; paintings, photography, drama, and the written word can stimulate, directly or indirectly, sensual images and thoughts. Erotic-phobics seek to censor pornography as offensive to community taste. But obscenity is in the eye of the beholder; to label something obscene is to reveal much about one's own hang-ups and limitations.

Many forms of erotic literature and art can express positive experiences. To embellish the erotic with aesthetic and intellectual tones can be captivating. What right does someone have to say that something should be banned because it is "lewd" or "prurient"? To view the nude body in the theater or in a painting or as a statue can be profoundly moving, a thing of beauty, interesting and delightful. Those who say it is "wrong" are venting their own hatred of the erotic on others.

There are, of course, critical standards that may be relevant to aesthetic value. A work may be badly done, without subtlety; it may be trite, a form of vulgar or ostentatious display. Thus one may bring the aesthetic judgments of criticism to bear on it. But, in the final analysis, if the consumer does not appreciate the product, it will not be purchased. Let each individual be the arbiter for himself of what he wants to see or hear, not the taste of the censor.

We perhaps should fear more the censorious attitude that represses our capacity to enjoy than any possible dangers of corrupting the young. Granted we need to use delicacy and prudence in exposing our children to the world of sex, particularly before they reach puberty, and we do not wish to unduly tempt or tantalize impressionable minds; but to keep them in ignorance and darkness is likewise pernicious. Sexual education for children about their own bodies and needs and those of others is helpful as they mature and develop. Censorship rails against sex; but we need an openness about and appreciation for sex. The unhappy and maladjusted person is often the affection-deprived child, the suppressed adolescent. How much more beautiful to discover love and sex as experiences of loveliness and joy.

One might add to this discussion that individuals respond to pornography in different ways. In particular, women seem less prone to voyeurism than men. Males apparently are more easily turned on by viewing the nude body or the genitals, whereas many women do not seem to be similarly aroused. Whether this is due to biology (different hormonal and cortical responses in the sexes) or to cultural influences is difficult to say. Apparently masochism seems to be a strong element in many women's fantasies. Tender sensuality also has a strong attraction: pictures of lovers that illustrate tenderness seem to be more appealing. It has been said that a woman's arousal is directed typically toward a particular person for whom she feels romantic affection, rather than tied to general displays of positions of sexual intercourse.

III

Eroticism has many dimensions. For humans erotic tastes are cultivated by civilization, and delicately intertwined with music and poetry, literature and art, perfume and wine, ambience and mood. The most powerful and direct expression of the erotic and the source of the most intense pleasure is, of course, in sexual orgasm.

For erotic-phobics the purpose of sexual intercourse is reproduction, not enjoyment. Indeed, as one reads the writings of the fathers of the Church, one hears time and again about the wicked pleasures of concupiscence: one should engage in intercourse only to produce children, never for intrinsic enjoyment. The church recognized that sexual union contributed to a conjugal relationship and was related to love between the parties; but sex was seen as a necessary evil, something to be suffered and submitted to (especially by the woman), never to be enjoyed in itself. To enjoy it was carnal. Our vocabulary is full of condemnation: any female who sought out sexual pleasure was of easy virtue, a fallen woman, strumpet, scarlet, wench, tart, Jezebel, slut, harlot, or whore. And males who sought sexual pleasure were fornicators, rakes, cads, lechers, satyrs, seducers, Lotharios, gigolos, pimps, or whoremongers. In total, such people were condemned as wanton, impure, lustful, bawdy, debauched. The term *venery* applied to all things sexual, and venereal disease was the most loathsome of all afflictions. Thus given our repressive cultural past, to free sexual pleasure from condemnation and to appreciate

its intrinsic value is still a high hurdle for many individuals
to clear.

Sexuality, of course, has a reproductive function; it
exists in most forms of life as a method for perpetuating the
species. In evolutionary terms it has a survival function. But
a biological function so deeply engrained in species reproduction has other strong psychobiological components: the
pleasure principle is one of these. Schopenhauer, given his
hatred of women, is hardly the best judge of the role of
sexual passion. The pleasure principle does not always
have, as he thought it did, reproduction as its main goal.
Indeed the stimulus to achieve pleasure can be so powerful
that it can move mountains or launch a thousand ships.
Moreover, of the innumerable times that two individuals
may have intercourse, only a relatively few may eventuate in
conception. Nature produces a surplus of eggs (approxi-
mately one per month) and sperm (tens of billions), which
rarely culminate in conception. Most of the times that we
engage in sex we do so only for enjoyment, and we wish to
prevent conception. Birth control or abortion can be
rational acts of civilized humans who wish to enjoy sex without suffering the consequences of an unwanted child.

But then again, rational human beings are constantly
able to modify their environment and their bodies; we
wear eyeglasses and false teeth to improve our natural functions, get face-lifts and hair transplants, are circumcized,
become voluntarily sterilized, and undergo surgery to transform sex where gender is confused. There is no strict
"natural law" basis to sex and morality.

Deep within our soma and psyche is the longing for
sexual satisfaction. Clearly, to reproduce and bear children
is not only essential for the species but a source of great joy.
Yet we also need and want erotic sexual pleasure: without it
we may wither and die emotionally. That is why the celibate

is profoundly malformed and sick, for his most primal natural function is being repressed.

IV

One may ask, What is the relationship of eroticism to marriage, particularly to monogamy? At its finest, marriage can be a source of deep happiness, especially when it allows for the expression of romantic love and where there is some erotic compatibility. But marriage does not exist solely for sex or love. It is the basis for the family, the conceiving and rearing of children, and the development of other consanguine relationships. It is a fundamental economic unit. It also nourishes psychological values, such as security and companionship, and enables men and women to share the many joys of life.

Under certain conditions, however, marriage may become oppressive to the parties involved. The high divorce and separation rates are evidence for that. The conditions of modern life are such that the original economic basis for marriage and for the nuclear family are often no longer viable. Not all individuals who marry in a fit of romantic attachment or for reasons of convenience can live together compatibly. Marriage may lead to bickering and rancor; from a state of "heavenly bliss" it can degenerate into a living hell. There is no guarantee that the tastes and interests of individuals will remain constant throughout life. Individuals may grow apart.

One might rightly ask whether marriage can and should provide the *exclusive* outlet for a person's erotic interests. Can one person ever fulfill another completely, or do we need to relate to many persons on different levels? Are we basically polygamous? The answer, of course, depends upon the individuals involved. For some the answer seems to be in the negative. For others, however, monogamous marriage does not seem to be a sufficient outlet for all of their erotic desires. Serious moral issues emerge, especially if the husband and wife are sympathetic, affectionate, and share common values. In such a case, for one or the other partner to experiment outside of the marriage might be considered a form of betrayal. Jealousy is such a deep-seated human passion that it often requires superhuman restraint not to give in to it. Erotic attraction may not last a lifetime, and usually does not. Familiarity all too often breeds boredom or contempt. Yet our erotic needs persist and we are frequently aroused by other persons.

There are alternatives to marriage that help satisfy these erotic urges: serial polygamy is the dominant mode in our society; that is, divorce and remarriage in order to find a sympathetic sexual partner and love-mate. Where divorce is legally prohibited or hard to obtain, there is great difficulty. No-fault divorce is the most sensible social policy.

Another arrangement is to abstain from marriage— and many people seem to be adopting this course; that is, they postpone marriage and engage in premarital inter-course, live together unmarried, or have trial marriages. Such arrangements provide the opportunity for sexual experimentation: if two persons are not compatible, they are not entrapped in a hopeless dead-end marriage.

There are other arrangements that can provide outlets. The oldest is the mistress or lover system. In France, where it was difficult to obtain a divorce, it was common for couples to remain together, with either or both taking a secondary sexual partner. Prostitution also supplies an outlet for those not satisfied in the conjugal bed.

Extramarital affairs are perhaps the most usual form of alternative behavior—the brief affair or casual encounter when the husband is on a business trip or the wife alone at home. Affairs of longer duration, though convenient, may lead to a split and eventually to a divorce, especially where a new, dependent relationship develops. There is always the danger of detection, with its unforunate consequences. Fear of being detected is a constant source of worry, though for some an illicit affair adds spice to life.

A great quandary emerges: Is it right for a married person to philander? Does he or she have the right to play around or wander off? Even if not caught, is it morally wrong to lie and cheat? Aren't sincerity and trust important? Shouldn't one suppress his or her erotic passions according to higher moral principles?

In recent years some have advocated "open marriage." Why not be honest with each other and admit when you are having an affair and with whom. Some couples report each and every tryst. Others engage in swinging by swapping partners or participating in group sex and occasional orgies. Robert Rimmer[5] has suggested that bigamy ought to be legally recognized: some persons need to relate to and be fulfilled by two partners. Others have talked about the need for a communal arrangement in which several couples can live together and perhaps share mates in an extended-sexual-family situation.

One should neither sweepingly condemn nor condone such experiments. Some people find it difficult to enter into such arrangements. It is deeply offensive to their sense of propriety. Yet monogamy is surely not sacred; nor is it necessarily sanctioned by nature. Indeed we may be more nearly biologically polygamous—more like chimpanzees, capable of plural relationships, rather than Konrad Lorenz's geese, who develop strong pair-bond attachments. In any case, we do seem capable of relating to several individuals in a lifetime and on various levels—erotic,

5. "New Concepts of Marriage" in "The Human Alternative" television series.

intellectual, social, spiritual. Thus for different individuals differing alternatives may be suitable.

Institutions invented for sexual mating and expression are largely conventional, and they can be changed, if need be. The point is that our erotic needs are such that they may not be fully gratified by the traditional monogamous forms; rather than be locked in for a lifetime, the individual should explore his or her options.

V

Another question that has been raised is whether sexual pleasure should be limited to heterosexual experiences and to the conventional forms of sexual intercourse. Penis and vagina, testicle and ovary biologically complement each other; and when they are brought together in sexual union, the act of intercourse is a source of exquisite pleasure. But not all humans find heterosexual coitus sufficient. There are a variety of other sexual appetites.

Oral stimulation seems to be a natural precursor to intercourse; other animals engage in it. Male dogs and cats will lick the labial folds of the female prior to intercourse, thus stimulating the clitoris. Oral sex seems to be an important component of sexual enjoyment. Anal stimulation and intercourse are found among animals and are common among humans. Thus the pleasures of erotica are not limited to the conventional forms of heterosexual conduct; there are virtually an infinite variety of sexual tastes that have been developed and embellished. Intense erotic experiences may take many forms: fetishism, fellatio, cunnilingus, sodomy, even sado-masochism and bestiality.

Homosexuality and lesbianism are also found in both human and animal behavior. It is possible to be aroused by members of the same sex. The narcissist masturbation phase can be replaced by powerful homogenic affection. There are those who consider homosexuality an illness, a form of perversion, unnatural, or abnormal. Yet it is a widespread phenomenon, found in many cultures throughout history, and apparently a source of significant enjoyment for many individuals.

If sex is not exclusively tied to reproduction and if its role is also to provide pleasure, then it is possible for individuals to find satisfaction in diverse ways. Aside from their sexual preference, homosexuals are not necessarily different from heterosexuals. They can be loving, affectionate, spontaneous, rational, and productive; they can contribute to society and lead significant and happy lives. Many creative personalities were homosexuals: Plato, Michelangelo, Leonardo, Tschaikovsky, Willa Cather, Gertrude Stein, André Gide, W. H. Auden. That our religious tradition has condemned such behavior is another sign of its penchant for repression.

The causes of homosexuality are difficult to unravel: are they genetic and hormonal, due to gender confusion, or to a fixation in the psychophysical stage of development? Perhaps in different individuals different factors may be responsible, though for many, homosexuality seems to be largely a question of conditioned taste. Many people are latent or suppressed homosexuals, but whether they ever express their inclinations depends upon social conditions. Few of the things that individuals like are intrinsically "natural": one may develop a taste for strong cigars and scotch, souvlaki, fudge parfaits, sports cars, water skiing, or scuba diving. Even learning to sit in a chair or on a toilet seat is acquired, not natural. The "daring young man on the flying trapeze" or the trampolinist are good illustrations of the fact that the body can be developed in different directions and that pleasure can be found in these developed skills. Thus homosexuality or lesbianism are for some an acquired "taste" that may not at first give satisfaction, but after repeated efforts becomes channeled as a source of gratification—much as marijuana may not at first turn one on and martinis may at first taste bitter, but in time may be found enjoyable. This pattern is true of most of our developed tastes, from the appreciation of chamber music or abstract art, to the enjoyment of pinochle and gourmet cheese tasting. Thus one may develop a liking for the female figure or the male figure. This is not to deny that there may be long-standing homogenic fantasies. Individuals may have the desire to relate sexually to others of their own sex, but these fantasies may be repressed and not realized until later in life. When they are finally expressed they can give relief and satisfaction. But the specific physical forms through which homosexual desires are expressed still have to be learned. Some of these acts may not even be liked at first; they may bring pain and guilt. Whether or not sexual activities are repeated and become permanent fixtures in a person's sexual life depends upon the *reinforcement equation*. Simply, if a particular form of behavior, be it socially reprehensible or not, is associated with significant psychological and physical satisfaction, then there is a tendency to repeat it.

Homosexuality does not necessarily involve the inversion of sexual gender. This does happen in some cases, where the male apes the mannerisms of the female, but the "queen" represents only a small minority of gays. In other cases, however, homosexuals wish to be, and are, fully masculine in regard to their interests and appearance. Even regarding sex, homosexuality may be an expression of masculine interests. It may be due to an overabundance of male hormones, not a deficiency. Making it with another male is not unlike playing football or gin rummy: it may be a form of fun and games. It also may be rough; there may be vigorous activity, heavy breathing, passionate embrace. The homogenic male does not necessarily take the passive role, nor behave like the woman, as is commonly believed. Homogenic persons with developed sexual tastes may assume either the active or passive role or position; they may engage in sodomy or *soixante-neuf*. In this sense homogenic sex is a learned mutual activity, like two in a canoe rowing on the rapids, or two mountain climbers helping each other ascend.

For some coming "out of the closet" means breaking through repression and finding pleasure and relief—but also accelerating latent capacities. But then again, any number of latent capacities can be developed and accentuated, for example, playing the piano, strumming a guitar, typewriting, or sky diving. We are not by nature fitted for any of these activities. There are capacities, tendencies, and genetic dispositions; but how they are tapped and exercised depends upon the environmental context. Homogenic preferences are resultants of a toti-complex set of causal conditions. Many homogenic persons are not by nature gay, but their gayness is cultivated, just as many other things in human life are cultivated. One can grow to enjoy sexual relations with members of the same sex, particularly where they are easier to pick up and more available than the opposite sex. An added spice is the fact that it is forbidden. There is high adventure in risk-taking and in doing that which is nonconformist or illegal. It is for some a way of expressing a heroic stance. Some may become political radicals rebelling against social mores; for others, newly acquired homogenic preferences are modes of rebellion, serving to express their individuality and proclaim their freedom against all of the social forces that seek to hem them in.

One point needs to be appreciated: oppression by society's hate has been a source of profound misery for countless individuals. Does society have the right to decide which fantasies may be acted upon and satisfied? The libertarian proclaims the principle of moral freedom: individuals should be allowed to explore for themselves their sexual inclinations, so long as they do not harm others. Gay liberation, like the women's liberation movement, is part of a movement for human liberation. This does not mean that society should condone flaunting of gayness before the young or advertising that it is better than heterosexual love. Yet, on the other hand, the banning of sex between consenting adults is repressive.

Self-hatred, feelings of inadequacy, a corroding sense of sin and guilt caused by social repression can do more to destroy an individual's happiness than virtually anything else. One should say to a repressed or latent homogenic person: "Face yourself; if you don't wish to come out of the closet, at least learn to live with and accept yourself for what you are, and satisfy your inclinations—to some extent —if that is what you need. Unless you are willing to do so, your life will probably be empty and meaningless. For if one dams up the call of the erotic, one is condemned to live the life of the damned." It was only a decade ago that the homogenic person was forced to suffer in furtive silence, to seek out straying eyes and find lonely souls hungry for erotic love and sympathy. He was condemned to loiter in dark alleys, public toilets, and gay bars, always fearful of entrapment and ridicule. Today, at least, there are more opportunities to find outlets and to meet kindred persons. The homogenic person thus has a double battle: facing his own internal fears as he tries to define himself, and his shame at social disapproval. To overcome both is to become a new person, made whole with dignity.

There is perhaps a wider source of sexual feeling than the traditional heterosexual and homosexual classifications would allow. I refer here to *bisexuality*, which seems to be finding increasing expression today. Bisexuality is the ability for individuals to be aroused erotically—in degrees —by both females and males. Are humans by nature bisexual, capable under certain conditions of responding in either direction? Some psychiatrists claim that one is either predominantly heterosexual or homosexual and that it is inaccurate to speak of *bi*sexuality. Yet the psychiatric model has failed in the past; for example, the typical homosexual was held to be effeminate and the lesbian a masculine, "butch" type, and both were characterized as "sick." We know, however, that only a small percentage of homosexuals fit these stereotypes. Perhaps there is a scale of proclivity, with varying elements of masculine and feminine, although bisexuality may also be an acquired taste, cultivated and channeled by repetition. In any case, a significant number of single and married individuals—we are now discovering—are capable of responding erotically and orgasmically to both sexes. Indeed, for them it is not the sex of the person, but rather the *person* of the sex, that can be the genuine source of satisfaction and fulfillment. One can be enchanted by both sexes and appreciate the virtues of each. Bisexuality seems all the more appealing to many individuals in an age when birth-control techniques have divorced sex from reproduction. If the purpose of sex is not simply to reproduce, then one can share and enjoy it with both sexes, and thus extend the range of affection.

Pansexuality, perhaps, is a more apt term, for it refers to our capacity to love many persons, to relate and respond to them on many levels. It is an effort to diffuse eroticism so that it no longer is fixated solely on the genitalia but involves a broader pleasure-touch-affection scale of shared experiences. Life is seen in part in erotic terms, and one can open his or her vision of the human universe so that it has wider sources of joy. Pansexuality, in a sense, is the eroticized Christian principle of love extended to all human beings.

VI

A perplexing problem emerges that concerns the ethical significance of love and its relationship to sexuality and eroticism. Many humanists hold that the key question to be raised about sexual relationships concerns their quality and not whether they are monogamous or involve a variety of sexual acts with many sexual partners. They argue that there are important ethical standards that can and should emerge in human conduct and that these transcend and are more basic than either the existing legal rules or cultural traditions, on one hand, or the tendency to promiscuity, on the other.

What would some of these ethical standards be? For one, it is fairly obvious that an erotic relationship should be based upon consent and that any form of physical compulsion or violence is harmful to the person who is being coerced to perform an act against his or her will. Sexual liberation means that an individual should be free to express his or her own tastes so long as he or she does not impose them on others. Thus eros is best expressed in the context of a mutually consensual relationship.

Also, the relationship should not be simply casual, but more enduring in form. Promiscuous individuals, who herald the vigorous sensual pleasures of one night stands and who sleep with different persons every night, overlook this consideration. From the standpoint of our erotic impulses, one may ask if these encounters per se are intrinsically bad? Surely, not. A kiss or orgasm is a form of immediate experience that, if performed with the right person, can be enjoyable. Such experiences, however, cannot be abstracted from other life-activities. The casual affair may be exciting, but sexual experiences play a role within the larger pattern of one's life. One discovers that there may be greater erotic satisfaction if he relates in a more meaningful way to the person that he or she goes to bed with.

Thus, intimacy can enhance the quality of experience, and an erotic encounter can be heightened and made richer if some commitment or bond is developed. The point is that we ought to relate to others sexually as persons, not simply as objects. Sexual relationships that are brief and random are apt to be animalistic and automatic in character. Making it on the run with someone you barely know may provide some relief for pent up desires; yet a more complete rapturous involvement might be more bewitching and fulfilling, and voluptuous intoxication that has some depth, more satisfying.

If it is true that familiarity leads to boredom, we must also recognize that haphazard couplings are apt to be one-dimensional. To consider another person simply as a sex object, a plaything to titillate or tickle, to be consumed and discarded like a used beer can, is dehumanizing. But erotic sensations involve our most profound emotions. We come to need and adore the person whom we enjoy. Thus feelings of love develop. Erotic experiences are most actualizing when they occur in the context of a loving relationship. Romantic love, at first, is a kind of madness; as it builds up, our infatuation may overwhelm us and we may become enthralled, possessed. Love is perhaps the most beautiful and powerful of human emotions; however, it must involve intimacy, commitment, and permanence to survive.

One should not, however, overstate the case for love. Poets and lyricists mistakenly believe love to be the same thing as happiness, but human beings need more than love: one can be swallowed up as a person if love dominates all. Yet surely love adds vital and essential elements to the good life. If consummated, love can bring to fruition our deepest passions and desires and make us alive. The whole world takes on new qualities for two lovers: nothing but love matters. Not to have experienced it is to have missed much in life.

In a situation of genuine love an important set of values appears: sincerity, trust, and honesty. Adultery is clearly immoral when such a relationship develops. Where there is genuine, reciprocal love, our obligation and duty is to be truthful to our vows to our lover, if we have given them; under such conditions, there is no greater immorality than infidelity, no hurt so deep as love betrayed.

It is when such romantic attachment no longer dominates and the erotic impulses are thwarted that, in a sense, one's moral obligation is lessened. In such a situation one may opt either to tell or not to tell the other. If one takes the course of openness, one is truthful; yet truthfulness may end the relationship, which may still have some significant value and which one may still wish to preserve. Thus one may conclude that it is better to be silent about one's extramarital affairs.

The key question here concerns the kind of relationship that is at stake: a lover, husband, or wife does not *own* the other person. Possessiveness is destructive. The right to privacy ought to be respected. A marriage contract should not mean that one forever barters away his or her right to the erotic; it should be limited in what it requires. Thus we ought to retain our individuality even though we live with another; we cannot limit ourselves exclusively to another. One may love another person, have a deep and abiding relationship, and a sense of primary commitment. One may enjoy erotic moments with that person, but this may not be enough. I may conclude that it is better to engage in extramarital affairs than to burn in silent desperation. Theoretically I should accord the same right to my loved one. I want her to prosper and to develop as a full person. Hence, I will accord to her the same right to find erotic thrills with others, as I have. There may be an unstated general understanding between us that we will do so on occasion, not promiscuously, and without knowledge by the partner of the identity of the other party involved. We face a profound moral dilemma: there may be a deep-seated psychological fear that I will lose my loved one if I permit her to transgress—yet never to do so, is to be closed to the wider thrills of erotica. Life is short and the call of the erotic alluring. Thus one might decide that the best course of action is one of prudence: to engage on occasion in sex outside of the primary relationship, but with moderation.

VII

Another general ethical principle emerges here that applies to the individual himself: the need to develop some measure of self-control. The philosophers of Ancient Greece recognized that some temperance in our passions is essential if we are to achieve an inner state of homeostatic balance, and a rational person learns that some modicum of self-mastery and self-restraint is necessary for a life of equanimity. One does not have to deny that the enjoyment of eroticism is part of the full life in order to recognize at the same time that a life devoted largely to erotic pleasures can be, in the last analysis, trivial and banal. The voluptuary hedonist who focuses only on the pleasures of the flesh may be profoundly unhappy, melancholy, and in a state of despair.

I reiterate, the erotic is good in itself; but we cannot separate life into isolated moments of immediate experience. What we do has consequences, and we often have to pay a price for our pleasures. To take the erotic as the be-all and end-all of life may negate other aspects of living. We must ask how our sex life relates to our other interests. Will it, for example, lead to disease when practiced indiscriminately, or result in pregnancy? Some self-repression, growing out of intelligent forbearance, seems to be necessary as a therapeutic antidote to excessive hedonism.

The criterion of health is an important prudential concern, for one can empty a well by drawing too much water. This is the most telling indictment of the dissolute life: that it can be debilitating. To live only for erotic sex raises our threshold of pleasure in such a way that we may become jaded, indifferent, or blasé to new delights. We may become fixated on the sexual, blotting out and destroying other forms of experience—intellectual, moral, social. The libertine who focuses exclusively on sexual passions is much like the alcoholic who lives only for drink and is profoundly unhappy, or the philistine who never develops an appreciation for philosophy, science, or art.

Even within the domain of eroticism, there are standards of balance and harmony that each one can discover. An important consideration is whether one's erotic impulses enable his creative work to continue. Where they enhance and support it, one may be pleased; but where they impede or prevent it, one should rightfully object. A person who devotes his life to the erotic alone becomes its slave; his world is limited in horizon and scope. There are those whose lives resolve around the quest for new sexual thrills. They go from lover to lover, driven, as it were, by an intense desire.

Yet no amount of sexuality completely slakes their thirst, and so, day in and day out, they seek out new partners to fill the void. They give up everything for a few moments of orgastic pleasure. Surely there is something more to life than this. In time they will become tired out; eventually the lust of youth recedes. One may ask, Where will the sexual hedonist be then? Such persons may eventually discover, though it may be too late, that they need psychological security, which can be established only by seeking out lasting relationships with others. But even then, life involves more than achieving erotic relationships. It is far more serious than that; there are other calls that beckon: one's work, a cause, family, friends, adventure.

The paradox we face is that we cannot live fully without erotic rapture; but neither can we live fully with too much, for we become saturated and bloated, and we need alternative forms of action. To luxuriate or relish in erotica —exclusively—is to suffocate one's full personality.

In proper context, Venus, the goddess of the erotic, is most beautiful and we should adore her, along with Bacchus and Prometheus. Yet she must not be allowed to dominate our other desires and interests or to dampen our drive in a world that awaits conquering.

Part III / Morality

Seven / Love and Friendship

I

Thus far the reader may feel that I have presented the case for the self-centered egoist, the individual concerned primarily with his own creative powers, enjoyment, and sexual satisfaction. But this is far from the case; instead, I hope to show that the autonomous human being cannot find life completely satisfying unless he can relate to other human beings. Sociality is so basic to our nature as humans that unless we can share our joys and sorrows, we are condemned to lead narrow and futile existences. The purely autistic person has limited horizons. His life lacks full body and flavor; it misses the most important ingredient of the full life, without which we can never feel complete: *les autres*.

We are defined as persons by the objects of our interest. If our interests are narrow, then so are we. Insofar as we can extend the range of our concerns, we are able to expand the dimensions of our being.

There are several ways in which we can broaden our horizons. On the simplest level, I have already pointed out the need for intimacy with at least one other person. The fullest expression of this need is in loving someone else. Love can be possessive, especially when we consider another human being an object and seek to monopolize him or her for our own consummatory enjoyment. Here the primary motive may be selfish: we wish to be loved, stroked, and caressed, to receive pleasurable stimulation. But there is another sense of love: the ability to *give* love without necessarily receiving it in return. Here, we derive satisfaction simply because we do something for someone else, not because that person responds fully in kind. Possessive love is infantile. It says, I want you to love me, I miss you, or I need you. The ego dominates this relationship. The possessive person becomes insanely jealous because he believes that the relationship will be threatened if another person enters the scene. Historically, husbands possessed their wives, who were considered little more than chattel. For the wife merely to look at another man would provoke jealous rage. Similarly, women had a smothering attitude toward their husbands and lovers and could not tolerate any sign of interest in another woman. But matrimony should not mean the extinction of our personalities or interests in others as friends, colleagues, or even lovers—difficult though it is for most people to overcome the consuming flames of jealousy.

Many relationships are simply contractual; that is, we agree to do someone a favor knowing that it is good policy and that they will reciprocate. This is an important ingredient in a relationship; it involves prudential self-concern.

Yet there is another kind of relationship that is based on the ability to give of oneself without any thought of direct gain. This kind of feeling especially manifests itself in the relationship of a lover to the person loved. A person who truly loves someone would, under certain conditions, virtually give his life for the other person. He is willing to do things, day in and day out, for the loved one. No one compels him to do so; it is not forced but is an act of genuine affection. One gladly goes out of his way for the sake of his partner and does so because he wants to, because doing so gives him intense satisfaction. I am not talking about dutiful acts that are done grudgingly because one believes one ought to do them, but about freely performed deeds of merit.

I surely do not wish to argue that one should always act selflessly. Relationships are not one-way streets to be used by another for his own advantage. A person who does not recognize another's needs as a human being is destructive both to himself and to the other person. Indeed, it is the ability to share with another some loving devotion that can bolster personal strength and autonomy. An individual who has not developed this other-regarding love remains dwarfed as a human.

The sharing of a full life with another human being— as in marriage—can be a special source of profound affection. Granted that some marriages fail; yet where marriages are viable they are cherished relationships (for however long they last—one year, five, ten, or a lifetime). One person relates to another on many levels—not only through sexual passion, but also through altruistic love, the joining together of careers, the raising of children, living together and sharing a home, pursuing activities cooperatively, and so on. To be alone in life and to do things by and for oneself is, of course, common; some individuals do not wish to enter into relationships they consider confining. But to partake of life with another can be a source of deep fulfillment. If one has someone to love—and that love is returned—one can remove the mask he wears in the world, and he can experience the joys and sorrows of life with another and without the need for pretense. The ability to share intimately with at least one other human being (whether inside or outside of marriage) is a priceless adornment of the good life.

II

Another form of other-regarding love is, of course, the attitude of parents toward their children—their devotion and their willingness to make sacrifices for their children, even though the children may not appreciate them. One doesn't say, *I* am more important than my children; nor does one calculate what his children will give him in return—whether they will love him and appreciate what he is doing, or even support him in his old age. Rather, one gives of one's self without thought of gain; he worries about his children's health, education, and welfare. My family is a *whole*: I am identified in everything I do with them. My bounty belongs to them. We share cooperatively our food and shelter. My deepest hopes and dreams involve them. Their prospects for success in life are mine and their trials and tribulations also are mine. If my child is sick or languishes, I am troubled; if he does well, I beam with pride.

There exists, of course, parental love that is selfish. All too frequently children are viewed simply as an extension of the parent's self. Many parents project all of their unrealized dreams and aspirations onto their children. All of the things they were unable to achieve themselves are wished for their children; conversely, if parents succeed in their careers, they often want their children to follow in their footsteps. Such demanding attitudes are infantile and self-indulgent; adults who have them are trying to dominate their children. They require submissiveness and aquiescence. Where children do not live up to the parent's values, or where their love is unrequited in kind, they may be rejected, disowned, or disinherited.

A genuinely loving parent will attempt to do the best for his child, if he wishes the child to be a person in his or her own terms. Let the child become whatever he wishes. One may provide guidance and sustenance where it is needed, but if one loves his child, one should want him to develop his own unique personality. One can love his child even though one disagrees fundamentally with his choice of a mate, career, or lifestyle. One should make allowances for his children, recognize their limitations as well as their virtues, not demand the impossible, but love them for what they are. One ought to try to do the best for one's child, nourishing his physical and mental growth. At some point, however, one should let him go out into the world alone, to discover and create his own destiny.

To love someone in a healthy sense (whether a husband or wife, a son or daughter) is to want that person to flourish in his or her own terms and to develop his or her own autonomy. I am not arguing for self-sacrificing devotion beyond the limits of human endurance; nor am I saying that parents should give without limits to their children and never expect anything in return. Such a relationship would be debilitating to both the child and the parent. One wants his child to be a *mensch*; yet some children may turn out bad, become self-centered, be incapable of loving. In such cases to continue to spill one's life's blood for a good-for-nothing is the height of folly. We should do the best we can for our children; but if after all is said and done they are mean and inconsiderate, there should be limits to what we should continue to do for them. An unremitting giving without end may be more harmful than helpful: "my child, right or wrong" cannot apply forever. If parents have obligations to their children, the children in return bear certain responsibilites to their parents. If they fail consistently in their concern for their parents, the time may come for the parents to call a halt to their unquestioned giving.

As parents we should try to develop creativity in our children, to cultivate their individuality, assertiveness, independence, freedom. But we also need to cultivate in them the ability to relate to others. If we do not succeed in teaching our children to give love as well as to receive it, then we have indeed failed. However if children turn out bad, it is not always the parents' fault. There may be other influences at work: bad friends, poor schooling, different psychological tendencies and needs. Doting parents who are too good to their children often unknowingly ruin them. To give the child everything he desires may be more destructive of developing responsible personhood than allowing him to earn what he wants. To work and save, to plan and conserve are important qualities of character that need cultivation. To go overboard in showering children with favors, toys, and trinkets that they did not themselves earn is to spoil the child—at least it contributes to a distorted view of the world. One reason that the children of affluent parents often turn sour is that they have been reared on an immediate-gratification demand basis. The child never becomes the adult. The parents are always there to help him if he falters, to make excuses if he fails, to gratify his hedonic needs as he demands.

Such children, overwhelmed by their own need for self-gratification, are self-centered; they take everyone around them, including their parents, for granted. They believe that they can always count on their parents to help them, no matter what they do. But what they lack is the ability to give love, not for a reward or out of habit, but out of genuine and loving concern. The question of how children should relate to their parents is a perennial problem that all human societies have faced. There are societies that have emphasized complete filial piety. This is best illustrated by traditional Chinese society. The parents were venerated by their children and grandchildren. Their word was final; they controlled money, power, and privilege. They demanded obedience; if their children did not follow their advice, they would be cast out. In this authoritarian family the entire life of the child was often dictated by the parents, including the choice of a mate and a career. This family structure no longer exists in modern society.

At the other extreme there is the youth-oriented culture in which the old are abhorred and their wishes and desires ignored. The extended family was able to provide members of the family with many more bonds of security and affection; the nuclear family often has ostracized grandparents and divested them of virtually all rights and dignity.

It is clear that for healthy relationships children need to develop a loving concern for their parents, a concern that will remain even after the children have gone out on their own. The desire of parents not to interfere with the lives of their children, to avoid any suggestion of authoritarian domination, has had the reverse effect of emotionally starving the parent. And their elderly parents or grandparents, having little contact with their children and a lack of love and endearment, are gradually strangled by their need for affection. Children should—even when they are older—demonstrate their love and affection for their parents. In order to do this, they need to develop an appreciation for the fact that their parents are themselves human:

like everyone else, they have their own defects and limitations, their own needs and desires. Parents should not be placed on a pedestal as either models of perfection or as unquestioned authorities. Thus it is essential for children at some point in life to come to appreciate their parents as unique persons and to love them in spite of their foibles and idiosyncracies. To be able to assist one's parents, especially to be concerned for them as they grow older, is important not only for the parent but for the child, whether he be a teenager or a middle-aged adult.

Similar considerations apply to other members of the family, to sisters, brothers, aunts, uncles, and cousins. How sad that the ties of family affection have been narrowed and loosened in modern society. The nuclear family, divorce, and geographical mobility have uprooted individuals from the broader family. Belonging to the tribe or clan had provided rich soil for the development of the human species. Those who are cut off from strong kinship relationships lose a great deal: the wider bounds of joy and affection. Can the values of the extended family be recovered?— that is a dilemma of our time.

The family, whether nuclear or extended, has many functions to perform: biological at first, then as a basis for the economic division of labor. It is the psychological function of the family that needs emphasis as a source of security and affection. A basic educating force, the family provides the nourishment for stable growth and for the development of the ability to relate to others.

The best family, in a sense, is the egalitarian one. By this I do not mean that each member functions with equal power and authority. Parents have a greater role to play, and they should not abdicate their responsibility. Yet children have rights as well. Each member of the family should count for one person and have equal dignity and value. A truly just family is democratic; it is one in which there is an equality of consideration for each member. Individuals have different needs and interests, power and resources; and each family must allow for these differences. The family should provide the basis for the self-actualization of its members; it should appreciate common needs, but recognize diverse ones as well. The family can become a growth matrix for all its participants. But to do so, the family must itself become actualized as a unit. Its members need to work in harmony and do things cooperatively.

As this implies, the best family is the joyful one: a group that works together, shares defeats, celebrates important family events, exults in common pleasures. It is exuberant. How unfortunate are troubled families, full of hatred and strife, divorce and alcoholism. How damaging they are to tender minds and delicate souls. How beautiful is a joyous family, full of loving relationships, happy, zestful, overflowing with bountiful interests and affection.

A good family is active, involved, creative, interesting; it provides an environment for both individuality and sharing. It does not suppress Patricia, who plays the piano; Valerie who is into Zen; Jonathan, who loves sports; mother, who is constantly redecorating and has her career; or father, who is an active professional. It allows each latitude and quietude, while at the same time providing support and strength. It is open and flexible; the growth potential of everyone is at stake. It is a wonderous foundation for warmth, sincerity, closeness, loyalty, humor, laughter, seriousness. It is life-affirming, and a vital nourishing ground for the fuller flowering of a meaningful life. A person may be able to achieve a good life, even if he had a deprived childhood or bad marriage; but not to have enjoyed a family life is to have missed so much that life has to offer.

III

Blood kinship is a powerful binding force; it gives rise to emotions that hold humans together. Kinship has its roots in biology: sexual reproduction stimulates passion and love, maternal nurturing provides the milk to sustain the young, and parental care provides the psychological warmth and physical security necessary for the survival of the offspring. Moreover, the family provides a biological and economic basis for joint survival. Out of common needs grow the bonds of love and affection.

However, if consanguinity were the only basis of human affection, the human species would be in a bad way. The problem for society is to extend the range of affection and caring. Plato thought that familial love was so important that it needed to be generalized throughout the entire polis. He deplored selfish attitudes that reserved loving concern to those within the family. Hence parents in *The Republic* did not know their children and thus would relate to all children as their own.

It is the ability to care about those outside of one's immediate family and to build ties of friendship and congeniality that are important for human fulfillment. Familial love has its roots in biology and instinct, but relating to strangers can often present a problem. Sexual attraction is usually between those who are not blood relatives. But how far can the bonds of friendship and of moral concern between individuals outside of the family be extended?

Aristotle recognized the importance of friendship as a source of immediate appreciation and of lasting significance in life. One must have *some* friends; to be unable to relate on the level of friendship with other human beings is to lead an impoverished and deficient life. We may develop many different kinds of relationships with others, and on many levels. A friend is one whose company you enjoy, one whom you help gladly without any thought of return, and one with whom you can develop trust, sincerity, honesty. A true comrade accepts you for what you are.

Since personal friendship is on the level of face-to-face encounters, we are limited in the number of true friends that we can have, though we can continue to make new friends throughout life. Childhood chums are important to one's sense of well-being. Indeed one's peer group may be more influential than one's parents and teachers in developing values. Childhood friendships give meaning and depth in life: there are things that a child will confess to a friend but not to a parent. Exploring streams and woods, playing games, going through school, reaching puberty, discovering puppy love, suffering adolescent crushes are all part of friendship; children learn about life and the world together.

In a mobile society such as the United States, it is sometimes difficult to maintain permanent relationships. We do have, however, the opportunity for meeting many new people, particularly if we move about: colleagues at work, their wives or husbands, one's neighbors, members of the same clubs and associations. There are various kinds of relationships. If we are fortunate, we can find others whom we can relate to, who will become our confidants, our close and faithful friends, trustworthy and constant, and whom we can rely upon in time of need and distress. They may be schoolmates, playmates, teammates, roommates, shipmates, colleagues, neighbors, or companions.

There are important moral dimensions to friendship that, if violated, can disrupt the bond. Basically, friendship is built on a spirit of mutual benevolence for each other. It is a relationship of amicability, conviviality, congeniality, cordiality, and harmony. Friendship, to be true, must be based upon a general concern for the other. This means that a number of moral virtues are present: caring, honesty, sincerity, trust.

One must not misuse a friend to one's own advantage, though one will do a friend a favor gladly. Nor may one betray a friend, or else the friendship is over. Jealousy, pride, and vindictiveness are absent among friends. Instead there is a genuine concern for the other, an acceptance of his faults, and a joy in his prosperity and achievements. A friend is one who knows your faults, yet loves you in spite of them.

Some of our social relationships are disproportionate in terms of age, power, money, influence, and prestige; but friends, as friends, are equal. They do not erect barriers but seek to break them down as they reach out to touch the other soul.

There are some persons who are so timorous and diffident that they make friends with difficulty. Their hearts ache for sympathetic companions, but they cannot relate easily to others. There is also the extreme case of the friendless person who suffers a destitute life in sorrow and tears. How sad not to be able to make friends. How essential it is if one is to enjoy life.

We can be friends with members of the same or the opposite sex. Historically, men banded together in hunting groups or as warriors, and comradeship was essential for survival. Thus friendship, no doubt, had adaptive value; today it seems necessary for our psychic health. Indeed there remains a kind of masculine bond that remains strong. Men like to get away from women at times: to work or play together on the team, to associate in business or in the army. They seek private clubs or bars to escape. Women also find intimate relationships with other women, without male intrusion, sometimes desirable.

One may have many acquaintances, but they are not

one's friends. For friendship is a special moral relationship held together by empathetic concern. Like love, however, friendship is not a relationship in which one simply receives favors; one must also be willing to give them. Indeed it is the ability to give to another person without question or complaint, and to share life's blessings and sufferings, that is perhaps the highest sign of human nobility.

Eight / The Beloved Cause

I

Human beings cannot live caring only for themselves, their own families, and close friends. At some point there should be a broader outreach and concern. Granted that our first obligation is to our immediate circle; yet we should not neglect the greater moral universe.

First and foremost we belong to a community. There is the face-to-face social network in which we function on a daily basis, the tribe, clan, village, or town in which we live. Given the growth of mass society and large-scale, impersonal organizations, small community identities are increasingly difficult to maintain. Yet perhaps humans always need to belong to some community in which they have roots and to which they are morally loyal. The problem of morality becomes even more pronounced when we recognize that there is a need to develop a sense of responsibility even for those who are beyond one's identifiable community. How far shall we extend our moral concern: to our nation, state, race, ethnic group, religion—to the whole of humanity?

The test of morality is thus not simply how one relates to others in small group encounters—whether one is, for example, honest in one's dealings—but how one relates to strangers, rarely seen; or to the future, barely known. To claim that one has some sense of a wider moral obligation is a sign of the development of a mature moral awareness. It is similar to that point in the growth of the intellect when one becomes interested in a larger universe beyond the immediate present, or in the expansion of one's aesthetic imagination. A person's lack of concern about what happens to other human beings outside of his range of action is a sign of distorted development and moral immaturity.

The basis of one's moral outreach may be questioned; the question, Why should I be moral? is often asked. In my view, the universe per se has no moral structure: there is no set of absolute value enshrined in the temple of nature or human nature that needs to be discovered and fulfilled. Rather, the sea of human morality is open and unchartered. Morality goes hand in hand with creativity, for it is we who create our own moral principles in terms of which we live and act.

The touchstone of morality is always human experience as lived; and the goods, bads, rights, and wrongs of human life are tested by how well they serve and fulfill our aspirations and needs. We must grant that there are basic human needs that require fulfillment if we are to survive and function in our environment. There is a form of moral development that human beings go through in learning to appreciate and to be sensitive to the needs and interests of others. The nature of society is such that some rules must govern interpersonal transactions if chaos and disorder are not to prevail. These rules set limits and place constraints upon what we may do, and they provide some guidelines for choice and action. Yet there is an element of freedom and there are moral options that are open to every society and individual. This is illustrated by the wide individual diversity and cultural relativity that exist in moral principles and values.

From the standpoint of the individual, one may ask: What is the source of one's obligations, duties, and responsibilities? And from the standpoint of the society: Which principles and rules ought to prevail?

In response to the first question, I would suggest that perhaps every human being ought to deliberately break some moral rule (especially one that applies to oneself) at some time in his life in order to test his sense of freedom. Surely we should do this, not to increase the sum total of evil, but only to develop some sense of our own power as moral agents. It is we who should master our moral principles; they should not enslave us. And if we are to have some power over our own careers and destinies, we need some sense of our own freedom of action concerning morality. Morality has been taken as an inviolable code. It has been imposed by the sanctions of custom, the church, and the state. Morality has been used as an instrument of repression to limit impulse and eros and to protect society from alleged harm. The moral whip was used, in the infancy of the race, to tame the savage beast and break his spirit.

There is a profound difference, however, between a morality that is legalistic, absolutistic, and censorial, and one that is nourishing, encouraging, and fulfilling. Moral principles should stimulate human creativity, not seek to repress it; they should contribute to the fullness of life, not denude it of creative joy. The ultimate source of moral choice should be human experience; and its test, the consequences of the choice in action.

What is at stake here is the scope of morality. There are at least two senses: first, morality as it applies to the individual himself, and second, morality as it affects others in society.

Personal morality—in regard to one's career, creative work, sexual behavior, or quest for passion or pleasure—should be considered to be a private matter. Neither the state nor any other social institution should seek to impose a uniform code of values on adults. This does not mean that we may not criticize excessive immoderation nor suggest principles of prudence—only that we should not compel compliance with a uniform moral code. Tolerance is the key moral principle of a democratic society. One should allow individuals to express their tastes and proclivities as they see fit, though one need not necessarily approve and should reserve the right to criticize.

The most difficult question of morality, and one that is of proper concern to society, is how an individual's actions relate to others. We may ask: What is the basis of regulative moral rules in society? I do not believe that the traditional accounts are adequate, for I reject the notion that there is a moral order in the universe at large. The universe has no divine purpose that can be discovered; it is indifferent to the fate of humans on this planet. Whether or not we will survive as a species is of no moment to nature: it is of profound significance to humans. We alone are responsible for our destiny: "No deity will save us, we must save ourselves" (*Humanist Manifesto II*). Efforts by theologians to read a moral purpose into nature at large or to anchor morality in some divine reality is an expression of human conceit. The religious impulse mistakenly looks beyond the factualities of human existence for a deeper meaning. But the attempt to root a moral code, commandments, and injunctions elsewhere than in the soil of human life is an expression of a vain illusion. Those who attempt to ground morality in metaphysics often undermine it, for they go beyond human experience to sanctify or prohibit deeds, which then become absolutes. To be moral simply because the moral law (or God or the church) commands it is to act without moral freedom or responsibility.

Morality, if it is anything, should be considered a product of human choice. The theist, more often than not, is a fanatic in his dedication to the strict letter of the law: absolute justice, he believes, should prevail. But in so insisting, he is insensitive to the deeper nuances of the moral life. He is unwilling to deal with the concrete contexts of moral choice, where one has to decide between competing goods and rights, or the lesser of evils.

There is no substitute for moral reflection. When faced with a moral dilemma one cannot simply apply a general rule to the particular case; one has to work out a decision in the light of a full consideration of the facts relevant to the situation. In our interpersonal dealings with others— whether as lover, relative, friend, or stranger—we soon learn that there are some things that we cannot do if we wish to maintain our relationship. The rules of the game become fairly common knowledge. We know that we can't consistently lie or cheat, or use violence with those we deal with, or else trust and honesty will break down. The moral principles governing transactional living and working together become apparent. We grasp them and teach them to our young, who will in turn teach them to their young. These principles have a double root, in our intelligence and in our compassion. And if what we do is based simply on rational calculations of self-interest, without any feelings of empathy, we will in time be discovered by others, who will not wish to relate on this basis alone. *Both* reflection and feeling are essential in human relationships, not only for others, but for ourselves; they stoke the fires of fraternity, and they keep alive our commitment to meaningful human relationships.

What is essential in morality is some degree of flexibility. Although there are the proverbial general rules of living that apply to most human communities, these should not be taken as rigid or fixed. Many social and legal systems, and institutional and moral principles that are no longer relevant may disappear; new ones will emerge. Different contexts and cultures provide opportunities for the creation of alternative moral principles. The ethics of the Stone Age no longer apply to the Space Age, nor those of an agricultural society to a postindustrial one. The problems we now face were not faced by our forebears. Nor will those of our children be exactly like ours. Thus morality needs to be open to modification by intelligence. Morality is connected to our sense of power and freedom, and it needs to come up with new solutions to life's future challenges.

II

Let us return to our original question: Why should one have a concern for the stranger, or for other human beings outside of one's range of action? We should have such concern because, in one sense, no one on this globe is any longer a stranger: all humans now come, directly or indirectly, into the range of one's action; I affect and am affected by them. While this is true enough, the question remains, Why should one have an interest in and concern for a broader perspective? Why not be self-centered and private? Life is brief. Why not tend to one's own garden?

I submit that to be concerned with the broader interest —even from one's own private standpoint—is to broaden the definition of oneself as a person. To be loyal to a cause that outreaches one's own parochial interests is to widen the expression of one's power and perspective as a person. Unfortunately, too many individuals are overly concerned with their day-to-day cares of making a living and fulfilling their goals; as such, they are focused on a narrow circle of friends and colleagues. To take the larger view can be a source of enlightenment and freedom; it emancipates us from bondage to trivia.

One can share with others a dedication to a greater dream. One can live, in part, for a noble cause. There are any number of causes that we can strive for. They are as multifarious and diverse as culture itself: launching a crusade; feeding the hungry; housing the homeless; working for socialism, democracy, or world-government; campaigning for a political party or candidate; working for equal rights for women or minorities; protecting the empire against barbarian invaders and extending its domain; spreading learning and enlightenment throughout the world; joining the conservationist movement or the flat-earth society; propagating the faith; believing in UFO's, world peace, miscegenation, liberation, the Kiwanis, Masons, Holy Rollers, or vivisectionists; helping to stamp out smoking, cancer, fascism, or demon rum.

Thus espousing and working for a cause—whatever it is—is important for the person so involved, for it enables him to transcend his restricted values. To be interested in the cause of others and to wish to share enthusiasm with them is to contribute to one's growth as a person. One's private aims are surely worthy of his effort and energy, but the broader aims may equally have a claim upon one's energy. To be indifferent to the needs of our time and to the broad movements of social change is to be morally insensitive. Thus we need to cultivate moral fervor for the beloved vision of a better world; and "loyalty to loyalty" is itself a moral value, as Josiah Royce has pointed out.

I have known many humanitarians who have been passionately involved in social issues and who have labored hard to see their ideals fulfilled. Unfortunately, some forms of humanitarianism are misplaced, illiberal, bigoted, and they may do us more harm than good. How can we be saved from those who would save us? For as much misery in the world may be caused by the fanaticisms of so-called do-gooders as by those who would leave well-enough alone. We thus face a dilemma: those who have no sense of a greater moral vision are limited as persons; but some who do, if overwhelmed by excessive zeal, can be equally destructive. Thus, in appraising a humanitarian cause, we need to know the consequences of the proposed programs as well as the motives of the activists.

Some causes are so wicked that we ought to oppose them. We should always be cautious of movements that are absolutist or that claim to have final solutions. Life goes on, and we learn that there are few sure-proof solutions to any human problems. Movements that are hateful of certain races, classes or groups of people, that are full of rancor, that wish to destroy before they build, are suspect. Those that demand utmost sacrifices today for a future that may never come, or those that would entrust supreme power to any one group (or party or elite) in society are dangerous.

If there is any lesson to be learned from the twentieth century, it is that millennial movements, especially where they are intolerant and divisive, not only fail to bring the millennium but probably set back the cause of human progress. A genuine humanitarian movement should have a sense of compassion. It should be limited by an ethic of principles governing the means it would employ: it cannot simply be judged by its vision of a utopian end.

In diagnosing the motives of people who are deeply involved in moral movements, we often find that some of them are pathological. There are those who so love humanity in its universal form that they are unable to bear it in the particular human person, and so are all too willing to sacrifice the individual to the ideal. We must beware of individuals who worship humanity in the abstract but think nothing of exterminating it in the concrete. A good illustration of this is the terrorist syndrome: the willingness to maim and kill innocent humans in order to excoriate wickedness and achieve a better world. The paradox of moral fanaticism is the tendency to vindicate one's evils in self-contradiction. The terrorist is prepared to wage war to achieve peace, to abrogate democracy to preserve it, to use despicable means in order to realize noble ends. I surely don't deny that sometimes one may have to use force and violence in order to secure one's aims—but that should be a *reluctant* choice. We should not be corrupted by using the evil means available to us; we should not be too ready to resort to force and violence.

Those who are eagerly swept up by large mass movements, leaders and followers alike, seem to have a superabundance of zeal and passion. But there may be a variety of questionable motives for their dedication: empty personal lives, banal and trivial (the fascists); sexual repression (religious crusaders); rebellion against parents or elders (revolutionaries). In each case they may be acting out their vengeances in the name of the cause. Not the least of motives are those of power or personal fame, prestige, and recognition. There are those who care less about the cause than about their own self-gain.

There are some causes that are generally limited in

their ideals, especially those that set nations, races, or ethnic groups against each other. We do, or perhaps we should, have some allegiance to our own national, religious, or ethnic roots. Each culture needs to have its place in the sun. Individuals are defined by linguistic symbols and values imbibed from their ethnic group. But these should not be allowed to imprison one. A more universalistic outlook is desirable. We should be able to find many forms of cultural life enriching, to tolerate and appreciate qualitative diversity—providing, that is, that the wider cause of humanity is not overshadowed by our devotion to ethnicity.

One should also guard against the doomsday pessimists who cannot enjoy this life for worry about the next. These are the critics who so hate present society because they think it so unjust that they cannot abide any exception to their indictment, nor admit that there can be any genuine progress. Such utopianists are often closet hedonic-phobics. They are unable to find pleasure in their world because it falls short of their impossible dream. They are self-denying secular priests devoted to a vision. Though they claim to love life and humanity, they are infected by a venom against both; they fail to see the possible joys before them, because they are blinded by life's sorrows.

But a utopian tomorrow may never come, for life always has its injustices and imperfections. There are times that are bad and times that are good, but never times that are perfect. Society goes from one problem to the next, whether depression, social conflict, or war. The utopianist can never enjoy life fully—not in Egypt, nor in Athens in the Golden Age, nor during the Renaissance or the Enlightenment, not today nor even tomorrow—for ideal perfection is always yet to be achieved.

I believe, in contrast, that we need a joyful humanism, not a pessimistic one. We need to have humanitarian concern and to work for the common good. Yet, life is short, and one should not squander opportunities for exuberance. A genuine moral altruism should have a double focus: there should be concern for one's own good, but there should also be a loving concern, a sense of benevolence and sympathy, for others. We need a humanitarianism that is positive and wholesome, that believes in both humanity and the human person, that is not willing to compromise moral standards in the process, that is entranced by the ideal possibilities of a better world and is willing to work constructively for them.

I should add that even though one may dedicate one's life to a cause, this should not blot out other aspects of one's life; nor should all of one's private needs be sacrificed in the process. If Moses had lived to see the Children of Israel reach the Promised Land, there might have been other tasks in his life besides deliverance. One should be prepared to take up new interests. One's whole personality should not be bartered to the cause; one should reserve some domain for personal dreams and enjoyments. One should not abandon oneself entirely. If the cause is worthy, it should not destroy but fulfill individual personhood.

Being devoted to a cause or causes is part of living the full life; for it takes us beyond our narrow limits. It is interesting and exciting to work for the cause. We are involved, not for our own sake, but for the sake of the greater good. And in this sense there is a positive qualitative dimension that is contributed to one's life. But the cause should not itself undermine one's capacity for happiness.

At the present moment in human history, there are any number of moral causes that might well concern intelligent and compassionate people. But we must distinguish a rational humanitarian concern from mere do-goodism. Often the emotional humanitarian allows his feelings to

color the facts, his compassion to overwhelm his intelligence. One should be committed to a general benevolence
toward all humans and do what one can, within reason, to
alleviate suffering and to improve the lot of all. But this
doesn't imply a blind devotion to the underdog or the naive
view that if only social conditions were changed, all people
would be kind, sympathetic, charitable, and industrious.

One should be willing to modify or abandon one's political or economic views if the evidence warrants it. There is
nothing so vulgar as a lifelong commitment to a political
party. To be a rock-ribbed Republican all of one's life is a
sign of pure Babbittry, but so is being a staunch Democrat
or a dedicated member of the British Labor, Conservative,
or Communist Parties. An inflexible commitment to "liber-
alism," "conservatism," or "radicalism" can be an expression of an intransigent faith. There is a kind of insularity to
the person so devoted to a cause that he thinks that only
those who agree with him, pay dues to the same club, or go
to the same church are virtuous, and that those who are on
the opposite side of the fence are ignorant, wicked, or
corrupt.

Moral righteousness and political wisdom are not the
exclusive domain of any one faction in society. It is naive to
believe that those who share my moral principles and
ideals and are involved in my causes are necessarily better
than those who are not.

True, one *believes* in one's principles and strives for the
success of one's causes. One has some reason to believe that
the increase in knowledge and enlightenment is a good
thing and that there is a progressive process in which we can
shed worn-out illusions, eradicate injustices, and achieve a
better world. Yet, at the same time, we need to recognize
that even the so-called incorruptible may be corrupted and
that even the most noble movements and institutions may, in

time, become sedentary or asphyxiated. The moral impulses of the first generation of fervent activists are often transformed by the second wave of true believers; then they atrophy in the process of being codified by the third generation, who are often simply bureaucrats. Thus one should have no illusions that once we have created a revolution, stamped out a practice, passed a law, or built a new social institution, everything will be fine. Only the socially blind will refuse to see the new problems and inequities that may arise; only the stupid will choose to deny them. One should be committed to the general cause of human progress; but he should not be so swept up by it that he becomes unwilling to dissent from some new twist or turn in doctrine or platform. In so doing he should not feel that he is a renegade or heretic, nor that he has betrayed his youthful idealism for the conservatism of old age or privilege.

Life teaches many lessons about one's early dreams. Not to dream is to abandon the whole human enterprise; yet not to recognize that our ideals are rarely fully achieved, or that unforeseen complications may arise that need to be corrected by still newer policies, is to remain insensitive to the nuances of lived experience. One needs to temper idealism with realism, a humanitarian concern with an intelligent appraisal of the facts. Even our most esteemed leaders may have defects; they too are only human.

One of the limitations of loyalty to sectarian causes results from their tendency to become divisive. We tend to oppose those who disagree with us, and this may separate human beings. We loathe to pay heed to what our critics say, or we are skeptical of what they say, or we suspect their motives. It is true that they may be wrong, and we right. On the other hand, however, truth is often a product of give and take; the sensible course is to leave open the possibility that it is we who may be mistaken, partially or in whole, and our opponents correct. Some critical skepticism, even about our own deepest values, is a necessary antedote to foolishness. The ability to compromise in life is a moral virtue that is not sufficiently distributed. We are not necessarily "selling out" if we concede that our enemies may have a point; nor are we inconsistent if we are willing to meet them halfway. For example, in whatever age, the critics of détente on both sides want nothing to do with compromise, for they think that to modify their position is to abandon their principles. But the political life is, by definition, the life of the possible, which implies compromise. The community is best served by the spirit of tolerance, and the negotiation of differences is the most effective method of social change.

I readily concede, of course, that some factions may be so evil that any attempt to reach a compromise may be venal, for example, the Mafia, or Murder Incorporated, the Stalinists, or the Nazis. Sometimes we need to act decisively; and the radical, revolutionary, or even the reactionary stance may be the only one to take. What we ought to do depends upon the needs of the times. One should be prepared for strong measures, even if they lead to conflict or violence.

Yet, in principle, particularly where there is some social consensus about moral ideals and principles, we need to meet our friends halfway and to endeavour to convert our foes into our allies. We need to recognize that our opponents may be sincere and well-meaning in their dedication to their cause, and we need to work with them cooperatively. Because we live in the same world and face similar problems, we need to work out a common basis for the resolution of our differences.

There is a tendency on the part of some humanitarians to offer oversimplified solutions: to attribute social problems to one or another cause and to think that to get rid of .

that cause is to solve the problem. For example, many liberals blame racism for the plight of minorities, many communists blame capitalist imperialism for the world's troubles, and many conservatives simply blame big government for domestic economic problems. But wisdom recognizes a multiplicity of causes of social problems and the need for a variety of solutions. There is a strong tendency today toward an excessive commitment to environmentalism—that is, the belief that *all* problems have an environmental origin and that if we change the social conditions, we will of necessity ameliorate the human problem. Yet some human problems may have genetic causes, or they may be due to defects in character. On the other hand, to blame all social ills on biological causes and to advise eugenic programs can be equally in error. Racial doctrines of superiority are despicable, but equally dangerous is the Lysenkoian view of social environmentalism. Both forms of faith are based upon one-factor theories—the tendency to find single solutions to social problems.

Related to all of this is the need to go on living in spite of the evil in the world. As I have said, there are some purists, who cannot rest content while injustice still persists. They will never find peace of soul or happiness in this life. But, as I have also said, we need to tolerate ambiguities and uncertainties, to be able to live in spite of tragedies and failures. We need to accept the fact that we live in a world of defects as well as of virtues. A resolute personality, one in command of his own powers, is willing to enter into and attempt to change the world; but he is not overwhelmed by the inequities that remain. A sensible humanitarian will work for a cause and will do the best that he can, but he does not allow the cause to get the better of him. Some skepticism should be a concomitant of even our most beloved devotions. We may never be able to get rid of all evil; yet we can enjoy life in spite of that. We should attempt to ameliorate social conditions as best we can; but we should have no illusions that we will achieve perfection.

Part IV / Death

Nine / Life Against Death

I

How should one face death? The ultimate good for each person and the basic source of all human value is life. There is a constant struggle of living things to thwart death, to stave it off, to keep living and functioning at all costs. Yet perhaps the only certainty in an otherwise ambiguous universe is that one's life will someday cease.

How should one face the awesome reality of his ultimate demise—the fact that death happens to everyone? Most young people refuse to contemplate their own death; they feel that it is something that happens to older persons and that they do not need to be concerned *now*. Yet at some point every person will have to come to terms with death. Indeed, life may not have meaning in a full sense unless and until we face death. It is only out of that existential confrontation that things are put in their proper perspective and one's sense of values equitably balanced.

Memory and reminiscence are the treasures of old age, when a person can get a better perspective of his life's projects. As one nears his end, he needs a broader sense of what life meant to him in the way of achievement or defeat, and he needs to prepare for his death. It is perhaps only in the light of a realistic awareness of one's eventual termination that his plans can assume their proper meaning, for in that light a person can distinguish between the things of true significance and those that are trivial. Many people forfeit their lives to banalities; they become mired in the inconsequential and are easily hassled about little things. They may be non-doers, bored by existence. Or perhaps they are perfectionists, unwilling to complete their tasks, overly concerned about details, forever anxious about what other people will say. They treat life as if it goes on forever. But it does not. Why squander it on trifling things, given the many opportunities for a full life and for creative activity and enjoyment? Life pulsates with too many pregnant potentialities to be wasted.

In the existential confrontation with death one discovers that the only thing that really matters is life. We should do all that we can to perpetuate, fulfill, and enhance it. Every moment of each day counts. My only recourse is to live with intensity and exhilaration—in experience, thought, action, and deed. My life, taken in toto, is my project; it is my own work of art. Every part of it fits together; its every pattern, color, tone, lustre, even its fabric, is of my own making.

Of all the species on earth, humans alone have a conscious knowledge of their eventual death. The question is whether an individual can face that knowledge. Will it overwhelm him? Will it be a source of anxiety and torment? Can life truly be said to have meaning if we know that all of our plans and projects ultimately will be vanquished?

In a sense, then, the first problem of life is the problem of death. We go throughout life resisting it. All of our animal instincts strive to survive, though there are forces around us that seek to reduce or destroy us. The body naturally seeks food, water, and shelter; it seeks to protect itself against the dangers of a hostile environment. We oppose any effort to defeat us, and we strain every nerve and fiber to live. To consciously reflect on our death—whether it seems close at hand or only in some distant future—is a kind of cognitive dissonance of the body, for the body has a whole set of homeostatic mechanisms to maintain itself.

Some individuals will not, or cannot, intellectually reconcile themselves to the finality of death, either of their own selves or of their loved ones. The thought that life will not continue indefinitely in some form is psychologically unacceptable to them. Thus there is a tendency to postulate survival of some kind. Indeed theistic religions derive their meaning and power largely because they promise eternal life. Religious belief has many functions; but the most important functions in my judgment, are tied to the eschatological myth, which tell us that death is only a threshold to another and better life in the future. Thus they enable one to escape the profound anxiety and dread surrounding death.

Many poor souls no doubt have been consoled by this image; it enables them to overcome the problem of evil implicit in the human condition: an infant is wracked by an incurable cancer, a youth is struck down in war, a young husband or wife is fatally injured, a noble person dies before his time. These are the tragic facts of death that perplexed Job and that have perplexed others since. The evil aspects of some forms of death are apparent:

a person may die prematurely, before having had a chance to complete his projects, or before reaching the prime of his life or the peak of his powers; or a death may be accompanied by torturous pain.

But, then, death at any age, even in the twilight years, seems tragic. It is not simply death, but the aging process itself, that seems especially unfair. We begin to grow old and decline; our skin wrinkles, our hair turns gray, our eyesight fails, our once-beautiful bodies sag and become deformed. We may not feel older at first, but the reflection of our body image in the mirror belies the fact. Eventually our powers begin to wane. We can't do the things that we used to without tiring; in time our energy is sapped, and we may become hollow shells. We realize that we won't be able to live on to see all of our aspirations come to fruition, nor to enjoy our children's children's children. How can we bear the thought that we will never again see one's wife or husband, mother or father? Aging and dying seem senseless and unjust in any form. If we were to remake the universe, we could do a better job—simply by extending the life span forever and by banning death. The religious believer refuses to acquiesce to the natural fact of death, and he postulates a diety who will save him. The surprise is that such an outrageously pretentious myth as immortality could survive for so long, especially when it is so full of inconsistencies, so primitive and fanciful. The chief reason for it, no doubt, is that there is a deep hunger within the human psyche (or for many individuals at the very least) for eternal life.

II

However, the doctrine of immortality is patently false on several grounds. First, what it promises is unclear. What is the meaning of immortality? Does it apply to an "incorporeal soul," as religious proponents have maintained? But the concept of an "incorporeal soul" is puzzling. The human being is an integrated whole: that which we call the "soul" (or mind) is a functional aspect of the *physical* organism interacting within an environment. Thus, it is difficult to know what it means to say that the "soul" survives the dissolution of the body. Notions such as of "disembodied spirits," "astral projection," or "nonmaterial souls" are based upon abstractions and reifications. Hume pointed out the problem of personal identity.[1] One may ask, Is there an independent substantial "soul" or "self" underlying my particular experiences? If my body no longer exists after my death, and if I survive it, will I remember my past self? Will I continue to have feelings, in my limbs, genitalia, and stomach after they are gone? How can I have memory, if I have no brain to store experiences? Will it be *me* that survives, or only a pale shadow? Antony Flew asks, Can I witness my own funeral?[2] As my corpse lies in its coffin, can I, lurking in limbo, view it? Does it make any sense to say that I can see, if I don't have any eyes to receive impressions or a nervous system to record them? Many philosophers thus find linguistic ambiguities in saying that a separate "soul" can survive the body. There is a basic logical puzzle in attempting to introduce a concept that has little identifiable referent.

St. Paul and others make a broader claim, however—that at some point in the future there will be a physical resurrection of the whole body, and not simply the separable soul.[3] This belief raises a still more serious question: What is the *evidence* for the belief that I survive my death (whether as a separable soul or by being resurrected in one piece)? For a truth claim is being made: that people who die come back at some time in some form or another, or that at

1. David Hume, *A Treatise of Human Nature.*
2. A. G. N. Flew, "Can A Man Witness His Own Funeral?" In *Hibbert Journal*, LIV, 1955-56.
3. *Romans* 6:5 and I *Corinthians* 15:42-58.

some future time they will be resurrected in a new guise.

Many cultures and individuals have no doubt believed that something survives the physical death of the body. Yet, as far as I can tell, we have been unable, in the entire history of humanity, to find sufficient evidence for this assertion. When I speak of evidence I am not talking about hearsay or old wives' tales, unsubstantiated reports by the uninformed or the credulous, but about hard data. Here I am asking for objectively confirmable evidence. What would constitute a test? The ability of the dead to communicate with, or influence, the living, or to have some observable effect on our experience would establish the fact. But I don't find the so-called data of psychical research in any sense conclusive. One might claim that we cannot decisively confirm the fact of existence after death *until* one dies and finds out; but if so, we ought at least to suspend judgment until that time— though it would seem to me that what we know about human and animal death as a biochemical phenomenon makes the claim highly improbable. Of course, some parts of us do survive our death in one form or another. Although our physical body decomposes, our skeleton can, under proper conditions, be preserved for thousands of years. It may even be (though highly unlikely) that, much as urine is expelled from the bladder at death, some discharged energy remains—hovers, haunts, or whatever—for a period of time until the body is fully decomposed; but whether this discharged energy has personal consciousness or identifiable experiences is another matter. We would have to submit this to careful scientific measurement, and the existence of such energy or anything like it has never been sufficiently verified. Some have claimed recently that there is evidence of people who have died and returned to report their experiences;[4] but these claims are based upon a blatantly false

4. See Raymond A. Moody, *Life After Life* (Covington, Ga.: Mockingbird Books, 1975) and the work of Elizabeth Kubler-Ross.

definition of death. Obviously those who have been resuscitated were not dead in the clinical sense of brain death after their hearts or lungs stopped. What is described is wish-fulfillment in the dying process: as yet there has been no verification of survival.

A further problem in survival concerns the time scale. Even if energy patterns were to survive, it might be for only a brief time—say, ten minutes or a few years or, at most, a few centuries (as do the alleged ghosts that haunt English castles until they are released!). But the claim for *eternal* survival is unverified and, indeed, virtually unverifiable; for how would we go about proving that something that survives death (a soul or something else) will *never* become extinct? In any case, it would be difficult for us to date souls that we might uncover, even if we managed to discover an incorporeal-like "carbon-14" technique for dating surviving souls. If we were to uncover a very old soul, its age would not necessarily prove that it was eternal. It would have had a beginning (unless reincarnation or prior existence is a reality) and most likely would not have preceded the origin of the human species in time. But, more importantly, we would have no guarantee that it would continue into the infinite future, unless by *eternity* we mean beyond the categories of time altogether. To make such a claim would at best be a form of conjecture, not proof. Thus, the immortality thesis needs to be confirmed before it can be accepted. But it never has.

In the last analysis, belief in immortality is an article of faith, an inference from a broader view of a divine universe, an item of revealed, not philosophical or scientific, truth. It involves faith that a divine being will, in some way, either enable us to survive death so that we can exist eternally or resurrect the physical body and soul and reinstitute personal identity and memory, even though there has been a lapse of perhaps several thousand years during which worms have picked clean our brains, marrow, and flesh.

Paradoxically, however, the doctrine of immortality is not peripheral to belief in the existence of God; nor can it simply be deduced from it. On the contrary, belief in immortality is itself central to belief in God and perhaps even its chief psychological ground and justification. The doctrine of immortality is not so much a descriptive claim about an alleged reality, but a normative ideal that is postulated to satisfy an apparent psychological desire. Indeed, the God-idea takes on meaning dramatically *because* man faces death, and God is introduced along with immortality as a solution to the problem of finitude. This existential-psychological argument for immortality involves at least three factors: (1) a response to the problem of death, in this case an attempt to explain away death and overcome it; (2) some moral direction and focus for what otherwise seems to be a random and purposeless universe; and (3) psychological sustenance and support, giving courage and consolation to the bereaved and fearful, and helping individuals to overcome forlornness, loneliness, and alienation.

The critique that can be made of this argument is equally decisive. The doctrine of immortality is basically morbid. It grows out of both fear of, and fascination with, death. The believer in immortality is fixated on death; yet he endeavors to deny its awesome reality. This means a failure to face the finality of death and an inability to see life for what it really is. This attitude has all the earmarks of pathology, it puts one out of touch with cognitive reality. It is infantile and immature. It exacerbates an illusion in order to soothe the aching heart. Death is a source of profound dread. There is an unwillingness to let go. One hopes for an opening to another life in which all of one's unfulfilled aspirations are realized in fantasy. The primitive mind, not possessed of science, invests death and dying with mystery and awe. Since death is unfathomable and a source of brutal suffering, the eschatological myth enables him to transcend the pain.

This mood of denial expresses a basic lack of courage to persist in the face of adversity. The belief in immortality is a symbol of our agony before an unyielding universe and of our hope for some future deliverance. It represents the tenacious refusal to meaningfully confront the brute finitude of our existence. Those who believe in immortality trust that somehow someone will help us out of our misery —however long we have to wait—and that in the end, despite our present suffering, we will have a reunion with our departed loved ones. Immortality offers therapeutic solace. In the past history of humankind, when disease was so prevalent and the life span so brief for the mass of people, it may have made some sense. Life was often "nasty, brutish, and short"; three score and ten years was not the norm but the exception. Thus, the believer in immortality has forsaken full moral responsibility, for he is unwilling to take his own destiny into his hands. A key objection, therefore, to the doctrine of immortality is its undermining of ethics. One is unable to be fully responsible for himself and others, creative and independent, if he believes that morality has its source outside of man. The reflective, moral conscience is too vital to be deferred to the transcendent. We are responsible for what we are, and we can achieve the good life here and now if we work to bring it about. It is not fear of damnation or hope of salvation that moves us to seek a better world for ourselves and our fellow humans, but a genuine moral concern without regard for reward or punishment. The believer commits another grievous mistake: he wastes much of his life. Life is short, yet it is rich with possibilities. Those who are fearful and unwilling to master their destiny are often unable to fully experience the bountiful joys of life.

All too often, those who believe in immortality are full of foreboding and laden with excessive guilt. All too often the pleasures of the body are repressed and opportunities for creative enjoyment, denied. Many such individuals thus barter their souls for a future life; but if the promissory note is unfulfilled, it means that they have lost important values. In retrospect their lives may have been barren and empty; they may have missed many chances, may have failed to do what they really wanted; they may not have been able to seize opportunities because of a deep-seated trembling.

Many theists believe that without immortality, life would have no meaning. How puzzling and contradictory is such an argument. It is a confession of their inadequacy as persons, for it is, I contend, precisely the doctrine of immortality that impoverishes meaning. If one believes in immortality, then nothing in this life counts. It is all preparatory: life becomes but a waiting room for transcendent eternity. Thus, this life is not fully cultivated, for only the next one counts. But life per se has no meaning, except that meaning we choose to invest it with. It presents only opportunities, which we may choose to capitalize upon or to let pass by. Life is too bountiful to be squandered in hopes of a morrow that may never come.

Does belief in immortality satisfy a psychic need? Surely not for everyone. I have found that people without belief in immortality often fear death much less and face it with greater equanimity than those with such a belief. The model of the good life that I have drawn in this book doesn't need that belief. Those of us who are not believers in immortality are able to develop confidence in our capacities as humans, and for us life can be overflowing with meaning. We are not without "transcendent" ideals, ideals larger than ourselves—for example, a belief in a cause that will contribute to the ongoing human community and to a better world for humankind—and we can have a sense of obligation to that ideal that is as powerful as any that the believer builds. Indeed, one may even believe in immortality in a metaphorical sense: we are devoted to the good works that will outlast us. But we strive for them, not because we will be rewarded or punished by posterity, but because while we live we find these ideal goals worthwhile; they also give added meaning to our personal finitude. We need nothing beyond them to support or sustain our moral dedication. Both meaning and morality grow out of lived experience; and commitment to the good life, as we define it, can be a more powerful stimulus to life than belief in the traditional immortality doctrine.

III

It should be clear that our first commitment should be to *life*. We should be *pro-life* and believe in it as our ultimate principle. Does that mean that we should, at every point, do whatever we can to protect life and to survive as long as we can? What else is there for us but life? Thus we need to use our intelligence to create a world that will preserve and augment life. In this regard modern medicine and technology are vital: they have helped us to prolong life. We don't simply wish to live, however, but to live well: creative actualization is fundamental. It is not *mere* life that is valuable but a life of joyful experience, overabundant with interesting projects.

Of crucial significance to life is health, not only because it is necessary if life is to be sustained, but because it is a good in itself. It is, or ought to be, our most cherished possession. Yet there are those who continually assault their bodies out of ignorance, unconcern, or helplessness. There are several basic conditions that need to be satisfied if we are to be healthy. Although fairly obvious, they nevertheless need to be stated.

First, there is the need for proper nutrition. This means a diet that provides sufficient vitamins, minerals, proteins, and other substances. Many people have improper nutrition; as a result, their whole outlook on life is impaired. Modern society offers the opportunity for a balanced diet that provides the essential nutrients, though it also offers the risks of eating overly processed foods, filled with injurious additives and debased in their nutritional values. Medical science teaches us that we need to avoid deleterious foods, for example, too much cholesterol or white sugar. Related to this is the need to avoid noxious poisons, such as the tar and nicotine of cigarettes, excessive alcohol, or drugs that are debilitating.

A familiar argument is that pleasure is more important than health and that some people would rather continue smoking or harm their bodies than live a longer life. What nonsense! We ought to live, not primarily for pleasure, but for creative activity; and those pleasures that are unhealthy undercut any such further action. Thus, to continue to ingest noxious substances is irrational, though I grant that it is difficult to break a habit. But the rational desire for health, if strong enough, can spur us on. Strength of will and intelligent resolve are instruments of moderation. There is a constant struggle between the pleasure principle and the needs of the body. Pleasure is a basic good, but its demands must be balanced with the demands of health. Part of the great adventure in living is to feel the urge for pleasure but to contain it by confronting the wisdom of the body, to enjoy the flames of passion but not to be consumed by them. One should give in sometimes to the storms of passion, but hopefully without suffering too much damage to the bodily equipment.

Second, there is a need for exercise. I cannot stress enough how important vigorous exercise is, whether it be walking, jogging, swimming, engaging in calisthenics, playing sports, doing rugged physical labor, or sometime else. I am always amazed to meet people who don't exercise. They claim they are too busy. My reply is that one needs to take the time—much as we do to urinate, defecate, copulate, and sleep. The body is a delicate mechanism; to use it improperly is to risk inefficiency and breakdown. Exercise is the best lubricant for the body. Some people claim that it is too difficult to exercise. They say that they are too tired or lazy. Exercising may be hard at first. One needs willpower and perseverance. If one persists, in time the results can be dramatic. Exercise can make one feel like a new person, refreshed and cleansed, always full of energy, relieved of pent-up anxieties. In the long evolutionary process, the body developed as a functional instrument; accordingly, there are organs and muscles that can and should be used. Thus intensive and continuing exercise, every day, can often do more to restore vitality than any medicines.

The third factor of great importance to health is the reduction of stress, for excessive anxiety and tension are among the chief killers. The conditions of modern life are such that stress is a constant danger. Some people think that the best way to avoid stress is to retreat from the world of affairs. But one must learn to live with stress, not by reducing one's activities, but by developing a proper attitude toward them. There are several sources of stress: never completing a task, undertaking a number of things at the same time, excessive worrying about one's tasks, or self-recrimination about failure. I have found that some people who do only one thing at a time do not have less stress than those who are more active. One can do many things at the same time; many projects can compete for one's attention, without their being wearing. One needs to complete his tasks if he is to have equanimity, but some people never complete them. They are imperfect because of their devotion to perfectionism. One should do a job well, but to *do* it one should avoid excessive self-blame; if one fails, one should try again. A positive attitude is essential. One should not destroy oneself through hypercriticism. The key to all great accomplishment in life is the power of a positive outlook.

Some demur. They point to the mad pace of modern life and they advise meditation. Surely we can't be active all the time, they may argue; some contemplative reflection is essential for life. It has therapeutic value, and serves along with exercise as a safety valve. To engage in meditation constantly, or to seek mystic release, is to risk retreat from life and is opposite of everything that I argue for. Some meditation within a busy life, some repose and rest, is relaxing and energizing, but only so long as it does not become the dominant mood of response.

The above are preventive measures to increase longevity. We can also turn to medicine as therapy after we contract an illness or sustain an injury. The promises of medical science are impressive. It is possible to live a full life of four score and ten years, barring a fatal disease or accident. And, with proper health, we can grow old with vigor and grace—assuming, that is, that we have proper nutrition, minimal stress, continued sexual interest, and have creative work. Some scientists have talked about prolongevity, the possibility of extending life to 100 or 120 years, or more. This would depend upon slowing the biological time clock; and it may be within the range of technological feasibility. If so, we would have to change our attitude about growing old. Early retirement would be nonsensical if people had nothing to do after their retirement. People need to continue learning throughout life and to change careers. How marvelous it would be if Ponce de Leon's desire could come true, and if we could extend the life-span for healthy, productive, enjoyable living.

IV

At some point death is, of course, inevitable. This raises two further questions: suicide and euthanasia.

In my judgment, given the fact that life is the most cherished possession we have, the most stupid course of action in most instances is suicide. If there is any sin of secular morality, it is to kill oneself, for in so doing one blots out any hope for the future. I believe, of course, in the *right* of suicide: society or the state ought not to declare it illegal, nor should religion condemn it arbitrarily. It should be a matter of individual free choice. Humanists have argued for the right of suicide as a human right— largely in opposition to the church, which has opposed it as "contrary to God's will." To so declare the right of suicide is to resist a dogmatic and authoritarian creed. Under certain limited conditions suicide may be the most sensible course for an individual to take (particularly in the case of an incurable terminal illness of great suffering). The only act of suicide that is justifiable is one that follows from a careful reflective choice. Yet it is a final act of futility and particularly nonsensical if the person is young and healthy.

Inability to endure the blows of fortune is an expression of cowardice. It ignores the fact that life always holds forth new promise and that we should plan for renewal, not finality. What sense does it make to cut off all possibilities for future experience because one cannot bear defeat, the death of a lover, the betrayal of one's ideals, or failure of one's plans? It is much better to develop some fortitude and courage, to take, instead, a new direction, to resist being broken. When I hear of the suicide of a student, I say, how foolish, how tragic that depression destroyed him. Far better it would have been for him to live through it to see another day. Thus the person who commits suicide is not a hero; he should not be praised, but pitied. Nevertheless, we should have the right to do what we want, fulfill our plans and ambitions, satisfy our sexual proclivities—even kill ourselves, if we so desire. But how senseless to take the final option, not because God commands that we not do so, but because one then destroys the only thing meaningful that one has: life experience. I would say to the person contemplating suicide: How ridiculous to consider suicide as a viable alternative. What a blundering choice, if that be yours. One must recognize that suicide is usually not simply a rational act, but one in which profound psychological distress prevails. I would say that aside from one's moral obligations to others—if they depend upon one and if one's act would harm them—one has to adopt an egoistic stance: that *my* life is the supreme good for me, and that to extinguish it, though it may be a dramatic act, has no long-range value to me.

I am willing to grant, however, that under certain limited conditions suicide may be a meaningful option for a free, reflective person. The situation that I have in mind is voluntary euthanasia; that is, when the dying process has already set in, when there is no hope, only great pain, and when the end is inevitable. Society ought not to prohibit beneficent euthanasia: it can be a kind act of compassion to assist a person who wishes to die. I refer here to both passive and active euthanasia. With regard to the first sense, we should not attempt to prolong life by extraordinary means, thus increasing the patient's agony; but we should withdraw life support systems so that a person can die peacefully. With regard to the latter, we should actively accelerate the dying process, where such action is desired, by the administration of drugs. Voluntary euthanasia is an act of suicide wherein we assist individuals in terminating their lives, if that is what they wish.

But two words of caution. Medicine ought to do whatever it can to keep people alive, and heroic methods are legitimate. We should, at all costs, fight against the raging of dark death, never give up, herald life as the ultimate good. Doctors thus ought to be encouraged to persist in their efforts. If a person has a heart attack, suffers a stroke, or is involved in an automobile accident, we should do whatever we can to heal his wounds and to allow his life to go on, even if he will be crippled or disabled. Some conscious existence, even with pain, is better than none; and we should be grateful to modern medicine for making this feasible. In approving of euthanasia, I am talking only about those limited cases where the dying process has already set in—though even while dying life may have some significance, for we can still see our loved ones and carry on to some extent. Dying is itself a part of a person's life experience, and we may wish to see it through to the dramatic end. It is only in cases where the patient suffers unbearably that an act of voluntary euthanasia is a meaningful option. In that case, since all of one's plans and projects are ending, one may decide to spare himself and those about him further suffering and anguish.

V

Should a person be told that he is dying? Yes, if he wants to know and is strong enough to bear the knowledge. We have the right to experience our death as a part of our life drama. We have nothing to fear of death—if there is no pain—since there is no afterlife. We will feel sorrow in leaving such an exciting world (particularly if our death is premature). But dying is part of the spectacle of living. One should be permitted to face it bravely. To withhold the fact of death, or not to permit one to discuss it, is an indignity against the human spirit. To be forced to die in a hospital, to be condemned to spend one's last hours and days alone in impersonal surroundings is cruel. I should be allowed, if I so wish, to pass away with my cherished relatives and friends in sight, to have one last glimpse of the beautiful world.

No doubt I will have my regrets about the things I did not do, those I may have hurt, egregious mistakes and blunders I may have made; but I also will have my memories of love, affection, friendship, creative activity, achievement, exhilaration, joy, and exuberance. And with tears in my eyes I will leave, perhaps even with my fists clenched. But if I have lived fully, bursting at the seams, finally, when there is no energy or vitality left, I will say to others in departing, "How marvelous it has been, and how sad that you have not found the key." Happiness is within our grasp. Life, no matter how long, is too short; yet I will bear death with courage and pathos. And perhaps, if I am fortunate, I can say: I loved life, and I did not waste it. It was wonderful while it lasted.

In Summation

What is Happiness?

We have been concerned with the question: What is the good life, and is it achievable? People have long sought for happiness, and they have explored the ends of the earth for its realization, but in different ways: the quest for the Holy Grail; a life of service; the delights of pleasure and sensual consummation, or of quiet withdrawal.

Happiness is, no doubt, available in many forms; different individuals and cultures have endowed diverse objects with value. I have emphasized the virtues of action. Perhaps not everyone will wish to be *engagé*, fully involved, creatively exercised; they may wish, instead, repose and quiet, peace and security, a life of leisure and retreat. Yet, without overemphasizing the point, the very essence of life —human life—is creative achievement. Thus, I have heralded the life of the doer, of the Leonardos of action, the life of the continuing pursuit of new goals and of the conquering of frontiers. We are defined as persons by the plans and projects that we initiate and fulfill in the world. The humanist saint is Prometheus, not Christ; the activist, not the passivist; the skeptic, not the believer; the creator, not the conniver.

As I see it, creative achievement is the very heart of the human enterprise. It typifies the human species as it has evolved, particularly over the past forty to fifty thousand years: leaving the life of the hunter and the nomad, developing agriculture and rural society, inventing industry and technology, building urban societies and a world community, breaking out of the earth's gravitational field, exploring the solar system and beyond. The destiny of man, of all men and of each man, is that he is condemned to invent what he will be—condemned if he is fearful but blessed if he welcomes the great adventure. We are responsible in the last analysis, not simply for what we are, but for what we will *become*; and that is a source of either high excitement or distress.

The human species is biologically determined, in part, by its genetic inheritance, which is the result of a long process of evolution. But we are also social animals and culture builders, and it is in the creation of the arts of civilization that we truly express our potential natures. It is central to the nature of man that we can—within limits— recreate and redefine our culture and even our biological structure. By means of technology and science we are constantly transforming our biology: by surgical operations, optometry, and dentistry we improve our organs and functions; and by medicine and culture we modify even our sexuality. We build a world, not only to nourish and protect our bodies, but also to extend and enhance our desires and ideals.

There are those, of course, who add not one whit to the fund of human knowledge or to the enterprise of life, but who feed on others; they are afraid to discover or dream. They merely go through life as passive consumers or delicate fawners. They wish to contemplate or accept the universe, not remake it according to their interests. But the key to human life is precisely its ingenuity and its inventiveness. This is the essence of human culture; and the life of the doer and the maker, the dreamer and the innovator, the hero and the artist expresses the deepest thrill of human exploration: the experience of creating something new.

There are all too few individuals who have the audacity to follow their visions—in spite of the forces in the world that seek to destroy these visions—who will neither give in nor retreat, but who will seek to add something to the world. Human life is as much a part of reality as is anything else: and what we want and feel, think and imagine, create and do is as important for our destiny as other kinds of existence. We can change nature, though we are of it; and our ability to restructure nature is as natural as anything else. Nature is not sacred, nor immune to change. It is constantly being modified by blind and unconscious forces: the winds and the rain assault the terrain; plants and animals feed upon the land and upon each other. There are those who say that it is evil for man to modify the natural ecology, as if it were some holy shrine beyond transformation. But to live is to modify nature and life in some way; we cannot avoid doing so. Everything that we do has a transforming effect. There are those who wish to flee from urban life and technology back to a rural, so-called idyllic, existence. However, they fail to appreciate the fact that the introduction of agriculture was itself a rude shock to nature, for it felled the trees and cleared the jungles, domesticated the animals, and bred new forms of plant life. To retreat to nature, even if we could, is to return to life as it was in the neolithic age, when man was a hunter and nomad who lived in caves and trees. We cannot turn back or abandon our efforts; we can only move ahead. To build the Pantheon or the Taj Mahal is to hew rock out of the quarries and to change nature. Art adds to nature; technology is the purest art of civilized life.

Granted that our technology should not destroy the natural balance in nature, do irreparable damage to the ecology, or so pollute the atmosphere and waterways as to render life impossible. We need to modify our goals in terms of their consequences, and if the consequences are harmful, to correct our mistakes. But we have to guard against a new ecological religiosity that idealizes repose and rest, sanctifies nature as it is, and demeans human adventure and change.

The tasks that emerge in human civilization are for each individual and each society to forge his, or its, own destiny. Human life has no meaning independent of itself. There is no cosmic force or deity to give it meaning or significance. There is no ultimate destiny for man. Such a belief is an illusion of humankind's infancy. The meaning of life is what we choose to give it. Meaning grows out of human purposes alone. Nature provides us with an infinite range of opportunities, but it is only our vision and our action that select and realize those that we desire.

Thus the good life is achieved, invented, fashioned in an active life of enterprise and endeavor. But whether or not an individual chooses to enter into the arena depends upon him alone. Those who do can find it energizing, exhilarating, full of triumph and satisfaction. In spite of failures, setbacks, suffering, and pain, life can be fun.

To achieve the good life is an accomplishment. It involves the development of skills, the proper attitude, and intelligence. It involves the destruction of fantasies about nature and life and the cultivation of the pagan excellences. The first humanist virtue, as we have seen, is the development of one's own sense of power—of the belief that we *can* do something, that we *can* succeed, that our own preparations and efforts *will* pay off. The courage to excel—the courage to become what we want, to realize what we will— is essential. It is in the process of attainment that we thrive: Sisyphus is not to be condemned; there are always new mountains to climb, new stones to heave; and they are never the same.

However, in order to have a sense of our own self-power, it is necessary to be able to live in an ambiguous world of indeterminacy and contingency. Nature is not fixed, nor is our destiny preplanned. We can build new monuments and discover new theorems; there are new worlds to be conquered and created. We must not let ourselves be mastered by events, but we must master them— as far as we can—without fear or recrimination.

If cowardice and fear are our nemesis, so are gullibility and nincompoopery, which must be controlled by the use of reason. To use reason is to demand evidence for our beliefs, and to suspend belief wherever we do not have adequate grounds for it; it requires that we not be deluded by the purveyors of false wares, but that we base our desires, as far as possible, upon the reasonable grounds of practiced reflection. There is a constant tendency to fly from reason to a paradise of perfection or quietude. There is no easy salvation for humans, and it is a delusion to think that we can find it. Life is restless and outgoing. It can never be content with what is; it is always in the process of becoming. It is the *new* that we worship, not because it is better, but because it is a product of our own creative energy.

Our actions are mere random impulses until they are organized in creative work. It is the unity of effort and energy that gives vent to our dreams. Thus the good life uniquely involves creativity. This is the great source of joy and of exuberance. It is in our work that we best reveal ourselves, not in idle play, or leisure—as important as these things are—but in the mood of seriousness. Yet creative work is a form of play and, if coterminous with it, can be among the highest forms of aesthetic satisfaction: planning a project, teaching a class, constructing a road, and performing a symphony are all forms of creative endeavor. Those who do not work lack the key ingredient of happiness. The "sinners" are the lazy ones who cannot, or do not, have the creative impulse.

Though the joys of creativity are legion, pleasure needs to be experienced and enjoyed in itself and for itself. The hedonic-phobic cannot let himself go. He is imprisoned in a cell of psychic repression. One needs to open the doors to the delights of pleasure to the many wondrous things to do and enjoy: food and drink, art and poetry, music and philosophy, science and travel. But merely to seek pleasure without any serious lifework is banal. And to focus only on physical pleasures—important as they are—is limiting. One needs an expansive view of life, to enjoy many things, to cultivate one's tastes for the variety of life's goods. Robust hedonism is a form of activism; the world we live in and have created offers splendid opportunities for our enjoyment.

Among the finest pleasures of life are the joys of sexual passion and eroticism. The celibate has committed a sin against himself, for he has repressed the most exquisite pleasure of all: the full and varied sexual life that is so essential to happiness. We must, therefore, be open to the multiplicities of sexuality. We ought to act out and fulfill our fantasies, as long as they are not self-destructive or destructive of others; and we ought to be free to enjoy the full range of pansexual pleasures, inside or outside of marriage.

Important as individual audacity, courage, intelligence, self-power, and the fulfillment of one's personal dreams and projects are, the good life cannot be experienced alone, in isolation. The richest of human plans and joys are shared with others. Love in its truest sense is nonpossessive, a cooperative participation; and friendship is the noblest expression of a moral relationship. We need to develop love and friendship for their own sakes, as goods in themselves.

But we cannot focus on inward ends alone, for the world intrudes in our domain of interests. We should develop a wider moral concern for those beyond our immediate contact, for the community, the nation, and the world at large. A person's creative work can and should involve others, and a sense of our moral obligations and responsibilities should develop that enlarges our horizons and enhances our universe. A beloved cause can give meaning and content to one's life. Though one works hard for progress, one should have no illusion about the possibilities of utopia; a willingness to tolerate ambiguity, even imperfection, is the mark of maturity.

Finally, each person must face death: life has meaning only if we realize that it will end. It is in viewing one's life as a complete whole that one sees it for what it is: what I accomplished and did well; whether I fulfilled some of my dreams and plans; whether I enjoyed life, made friends, fell in love, worked for a beloved cause, and so forth. I should have no false hopes about death, but I should do what I can to ward it off. Indeed, health is a first condition if one is to live well. We must not be deluded by a belief in immortality but should face death realistically. A free man worships the creative life as his ultimate good. But when death comes, he will accept it with equanimity, if with sorrow; and he will realize that in the face of death the only thing that really counts is what has been the quality of his life, and what he has given or left for others.

Thus we may ask, Can we achieve the exuberant life? Yes, to some extent, but not by following the path that most philosophers and theologians have advised. The key to a full life is to open up to life—not suppress it or flee from it, but to give vent to our creative endeavors, to allow our imagination and creativity to have free play. We need to have confidence in our own power and to live audaciously. We need to be critical and skeptical of premature claims of truth or virtue, to use our common sense based upon reason and experience. We should not be afraid to enjoy pleasure or sexuality. Yet, at the same time, we need to develop love and friendship with others and a genuine moral concern for a better world. These are some of the ingredients that I have discovered contribute to the richness of life.

Each day, each moment, can be an adventure, pregnant with opportunity. With so many good things to do and enjoy, life can be interesting, exciting, and energizing. The *full* life is the goal. Though one has cherished memories, one need not look back; nor should one remain fixated on the present, indecisive and afraid to act. We need always to look ahead to the future: life is open-ended possibilities. We are not only what we are now, but also what we will choose to become. That is the faith and the optimism that has inspired me. Whether others will also find joy in the strenuous life of challenge is, of course, up to them. It is there simply awaiting one's action. The point is that it does not depend simply upon nature or society, destiny or God, but on what each person chooses for himself.

DATE DUE